D1523361

# The Beer Cheese Book

# THE
# BEER CHEESE
# BOOK

**GARIN PIRNIA**

UNIVERSITY PRESS OF KENTUCKY

Scholarly publisher for the Commonwealth,
serving Bellarmine University, Berea College, Centre College of Kentucky, Eastern
Kentucky University, The Filson Historical Society, Georgetown College, Kentucky
Historical Society, Kentucky State University, Morehead State University, Murray
State University, Northern Kentucky University, Transylvania University, University
of Kentucky, University of Louisville, and Western Kentucky University.
All rights reserved.

*Editorial and Sales Offices:* The University Press of Kentucky
663 South Limestone Street, Lexington, Kentucky 40508-4008
www.kentuckypress.com

Library of Congress Cataloging-in-Publication Data

Names: Pirnia, Garin, author.
Title: The beer cheese book / Garin Pirnia.
Description: Lexington, Kentucky : University Press of Kentucky, [2017] |
    Includes index.
Identifiers: LCCN 2017032719| ISBN 9780813174662 (hardcover : acid-free
    paper) | ISBN 9780813174679 (pdf) | ISBN 9780813174686 (epub)
Subjects: LCSH: Cooking (Beer) | Cooking (Cheese) | Cooking, American. | Dips
    (Appetizers) | LCGFT: Cookbooks.
Classification: LCC TX726.3 .P57 2017 | DDC 641.6/23—dc23
LC record available at https://lccn.loc.gov/2017032719

This book is printed on acid-free paper meeting the requirements of the American
National Standard for Permanence in Paper for Printed Library Materials.

Manufactured in Canada.

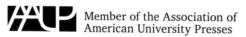 Member of the Association of
American University Presses

Dedicated to my parents,
Jean and Steven Pirnia.

I love you more than you'll ever know.

# CONTENTS

# INTRODUCTION

"Why are you writing a book on beer cheese?" people have asked while I've completed research for this book. My response: "Why not?" Not in a million years did I think the first book I would write—let alone any book—would be on beer cheese. Yet now it makes total sense to me. I discovered that beer cheese takes on a cultdom, and its fans are voracious. If you love beer cheese, you *really* love beer cheese. Beer and cheese and spices blended together—what's not to like? It's been amazing to learn just how many people do not know what beer cheese is, or how many Kentuckians are unaware that beer cheese was invented in the Commonwealth, or that a Beer Cheese Festival takes place in their state every June (see chapter 4). Why write a book on beer cheese? To educate the masses—both inside and outside of Kentucky—on what the heck this wonderful, esoteric dish is and why it matters.

My Kentucky story began when I was four years old, when my mother got into the horse business. She owned a few horses and kept them in Shelbyville. On the weekends and during the summer, she'd drag my brother, my dad, me, and sometimes my friend Christine to horse shows and farms in the region. I grew up in Centerville, Ohio, a suburb of Dayton that was a mere hour's drive from the Bluegrass State. While in Kentucky, we'd take excursions to Louisville, Lexington, Harrodsburg, and other towns to attend horse shows and do things like visit the Kentucky Horse Park and take horseback-riding lessons. For a few years Kentucky became a second home for our family. I probably was too young to appreciate the beauty of the state, as I was more interested in the free breakfast at the Ramada Inn and chasing after the farm cats. However, I do have a strong recollection of the undulating acres of farmland, houses situated atop hills, and fences running parallel to the meandering roads. I don't remember trying out the foods of Kentucky as kid, though—my family and I were too focused on fast-food chains, and I wasn't the food snob I am now—but we did dine at Claudia Sanders in Shelbyville, a famous eatery (named after the Colonel's wife) that still exemplifies what traditional Kentucky (and Southern food) is all about: ham 'n' biscuits, yeast rolls, sweet tea, Kentucky pie, and fried chicken. I loved going to Kentucky so much that whenever we drove home and crossed the now-crumbling Brent Spence Bridge into Ohio, I immediately felt crestfallen. On the way to Kentucky the blue "Welcome to Kentucky" sign put a smile on my face, because going to Kentucky meant a repose from our lives in Dayton. But being back home signaled our fun-filled farm adventures were over—and that I had to return to school.

My mom eventually retired from the horse business, so we stopped going to Kentucky as often. In my early twenties I moved to Los Angeles and then to Chicago, but after living in back-to-back stressful (and expensive) cities, the idea of living in Kentucky seemed exotic. Basically, I loved the idea of harkening back to my roots. In May 2011 on a whim I packed up my stuff and moved to Covington, Kentucky, where I reside today. Several times a week I drive over the Brent Spence Bridge and under that "Welcome to Kentucky" sign, which signals to me I'm home. Since moving to the Bluegrass State (and in writing this book), I've spent time exploring Lexington and Louisville and smaller Kentucky cities such as Winchester, Paris, and Danville. Kentuckians are the nicest, most hospitable people you'll ever meet—especially those involved in the beer cheese industry; they're always happy to discuss beer cheese with you.

I had no clue what beer cheese was until I moved to Northern Kentucky. One day, within a few months of relocating to Covington, I was in Party Town, a liquor/party store a few miles from my house. I noticed they sold something called beer cheese, which was packed in plastic containers and stored in their refrigerated section. I bought a brand called Kentucky Beer Cheese and instantly became enamored. Beer cheese seemed effortless to make, so I started making my own. This led me to enter my beer cheese in 2014's Beer Cheese Festival in Winchester. It's laughable to think of myself as a home cook, because growing up I resisted cooking and got irritated when I received kitchen

# Introduction

utensils for Christmas. Today, that's all I ask for. I don't consider myself a chef, but in creating this book I found myself in the kitchen experimenting with recipes, and it made me realize I had succumbed to my DNA. My mother, when she wasn't lugging us kids off to school or traveling to Kentucky, cooked and baked up a storm. She drew from her German heritage to cook sauerkraut balls; she whipped up comfort foods like beef stroganoff, scalloped corn, potato salad, and German chocolate cake; and she also made delicious Persian food. And now, with beer cheese, I finally could contribute something to the equation.

In hindsight, I now see the universe had been preparing me, for years, to move to Kentucky so I could discover beer cheese and write this book for y'all. Beer cheese is my destiny, and I hope it will be yours, too.

# 1

# HISTORY

For more than seventy years, the Kentucky River drew Johnnie Allman like a magnet. Even though life on the river was fraught with flood, fires, and murder, Johnnie and his family kept coming back to their beloved waterway.

Allman was born in 1906 and grew up in Richmond, Kentucky, about twenty minutes from the Kentucky River. His early career included working for the Richmond police department and the Kentucky State Police, and he also spent time as a lifeguard. In 1939 he opened Johnnie Allman's the Driftwood Inn on the banks of the temperamental river. The Driftwood, located on Athens Boonesboro Road, in Winchester, Clark County, is the reputed birthplace of beer cheese.

Johnnie's cousin Joe Allman was a chef who'd spent time working in kitchens in New Orleans, Arizona, and Florida, as well as wrangling a chuck wagon in the Southwest. When Joe moved back to Winchester, he worked at the Driftwood and pioneered his Kentucky River beer cheese. Called Snappy

Beer Cheese, it was a cold appetizer spread made with cold-pack Wisconsin sharp cheddar cheese (a type of premade cheese spread that comes in a tub), garlic, cayenne pepper, and flattened beer. The "snappy" part derives from the spiciness of the pepper.

Over the years the truth of beer cheese's origins has been warped, and tall tales have emerged. Bob Tabor, founder of Winchester's River Rat Beer Cheese, told me this: "One version [of beer cheese's origin] is that Joe, who had been a chef in Phoenix, came back here one summer and was working down at the river and made the first batch of beer cheese. So then the next question is: Did he create it or did he make it from a recipe that was given to him?" Tabor's version of the story stars a group of Winchesterians who wintered in Florida and hung out together. "One of these hangouts had beer cheese, so based on the fact that these people were from Kentucky, [the owners] let them have the recipe. I had this lady in here one day that swore she was sitting at the table when Ethel Stevens gave John Allman the recipe. So I'm thinking, well, maybe John gave the recipe to his cousin, and he made the beer cheese from that. The other story is that Joe created it. Well, maybe he created it off this piece of paper somebody handed to him."

"It was pretty much Joe's creation. It didn't come from Florida," John B. Allman, Johnnie's son, tells me. "It wasn't something he had copied. Joe was one of these people who couldn't handle success. He had quite a few restaurants of his own, and as soon as he'd get them up and running, I guess the challenge was done, so he'd move on to something else. He was quite a restaurateur."

And so was Johnnie Allman. The Driftwood Inn closed in 1945, and Johnnie opened Allman's that same year, at today's location of Hall's on the River. Allman's lasted until 1950. From 1951 to 1953, Allman briefly abandoned the river and ran Smokehouse, on U.S. 25 near the Blue Grass Army Depot. When that business closed, for two years he operated another restaurant named Allman's, this one in Lexington, and then he returned to the river. Allman's Fisherman's Inn/Johnnie Allman's operated from 1955 to 1978 across the street from Hall's.

"It was quite a place, the old restaurant," John B. says. They called the locals "river rats." "The employees were more like family than anything," he says. "Everybody spent time with each other rather than watching television. It was good times back then."

The restaurant served steaks and burgers and fish caught right out of the river. "At one time we had commercial fishermen along the river, and [the restaurant] bought most of their fish from the locals," John B. says. "There was catfish. They did real well with that." John B. occasionally would help with the beer cheese making. Back then they didn't own a commercial mixer, so it was

The Fisherman's Inn,
July 27, 1959.
(Courtesy Allman family)

all handmade. "We'd usually make up about fifty, seventy-five pounds of beer cheese every other day or so," he says, "and my hands would burn from where we put in the cayenne pepper." A couple of fires and several floods wreaked havoc on the businesses, including major floods in 1950, 1962, and 1978, the last of which finished Allman's praised reign on the river.

"We just bounced right back," John B. says about the natural disasters. "Sometimes we'd have a flood and within a week or so we'd be back in business. We had big trucks come down, and they'd load the freezers and every-thing and put them up on the hill and plug them back in and keep all the freezers running till the river went back down. We'd clean up and move back in with a bunch of fans to dry everything out." Tabor recalls, "I remember a picture of John Allman one year in the flood, standing out in front of his res-taurant with his arms full of beer."

In 1950 Johnnie decided to sell the original Allman's to Karl Johnson. Rumors swirled that Allman actually lost the restaurant to Johnson in a card game. "No, no, that's not true," John B. disputes. "I don't know where that got out. I heard about that too, but that's not true. My father would never gamble like that. He played a friendly game of poker every now and then, but no high stakes. He wouldn't lose a whole piece of property. He just sold it."

Part of the transaction with Johnson stipulated that Johnnie would not open another restaurant on the river for five years, thus explaining why he operated the Smokehouse and the Lexington Allman's. When the five years were up, he built Fisherman's Inn on the former location of the Driftwood.

More drama flared up on July 23, 1965, when a man murdered Johnson at his restaurant. "The guy who shot him must've been [upset] over a gambling debt," John B. Allman says. "Both of them gambled quite a bit. This has noth-ing to do with my father, of course. The guy, John Stevens, just cold bloodedly shot Karl Johnson. It was an argument from what I understand. Of course this is hearsay. Karl told John Stevens to leave, and he said, 'I'm leaving, but I'll be right back,' and came in and shot Karl. He put the gun on the counter, walked around, drank himself a beer, and waited for the police. It sounds like it's pretty barbaric and all, but the river wasn't a rough-and-tumble place."

A couple of months after Johnson died, Gertrude and George Hall took over the restaurant and changed the name to Hall's on the River. By 1978 Johnnie had retired and leased out his restaurant. That same year a terrible flood destroyed Allman's, followed by a fire so damaging that the family decided not to rebuild. The foundation of Allman's remains and has become a relic of those decades-long good times. John B. didn't want to keep his family's restaurant tradition going, so he chose to work in construction and briefly owned a liquor store in Richmond. "I was born and raised in it, and I needed to get away from it," he says. Johnnie Allman passed away in his eighty-third year, on October 29, 1989, and left behind a venerable legacy.

In 2013 a piece of legislation further defined and solidified that legacy. Bob Leeper, a former member of the Kentucky senate, helped the Kentucky legislature enact amendment SCA3, which states: "Delete original provisions; create a new section of KRS Chapter 2 naming and designating Clark County, Kentucky, as the birthplace of beer cheese." The statute went into effect June

25, 2013. No other city in the world can claim such preeminence, thanks to the Allmans.[1]

John B. retired to Bokeelia, Florida, but his son Ian—who lives in Mount Vernon, Kentucky—considers maybe resurrecting an Allman's restaurant. "In the back of my mind, I wouldn't mind doing something like that someday," he says. "I've worked in a few restaurants around here. Right now the beer cheese is keeping me busy." In 2009 Ian and his wife Angie resuscitated the Allman name and began retailing the beer cheese. "There was a demand for it," Ian says. "People really liked it and remembered it from the restaurant. A lot of the folks my parents' age who remember the restaurant were really excited about having [beer cheese] out again."

Of course today the Allmans use a commercial mixer, which is a good thing because they make from four to five thousand pounds of beer cheese per year. Ian was six years old when the last Allman's restaurant shut down, but he remembers life as a river rat. "Beer cheese was something that was always around," he says. "I've never known a day without it."

He and Angie have tried their best to stick with the original, decades-old Allman's recipe instead of compromising quality and cutting corners. "It's more expensive the way that they make it," John B. says. "I guess that's what you get."

Ian and Angie use the same distributor of high-quality Wisconsin cheddar from Johnnie Allman's days. "Ian and Angie have been up there three or four times," John B. says. "They even remember years back when my people would order from them to get the base cheese. Some of the employees at the cheesery—I don't know what to call it—they remembered, so now they welcome Ian and Angie when they get their cheese."

Most modern beer cheese makers use Allman's recipe as a jumping-off point, but other recipes have germinated from the original recipe. "There have been quite a few changes with some of the people making the cheese," John B. says. "Now they've gone with a less expensive [base] cheese, I guess because of the profit margins. It's not the real thing. The way we see it, if they didn't stick to the original recipe, then it's not original. It's their version of beer cheese." Since 2009 a panoply of beer cheese artisans have popped up, but Ian says, "We're not having any trouble selling ours. I guess there's room for everybody. Everybody puts on twist on it."

The original beer cheese recipe is cryptic, cloaked in a mystery on the level of who really shot JFK. Ask any beer cheese maker their formula, and they'll act demure as to what's in their dip. Some refuse to confess what kind of beer they use, or where they get their cheese from, or what extra spices they added, or what process they used to make it. It wasn't always like that, though.

"Back when Ian's grandfather was making beer cheese, no one minded sharing their recipe if someone asked, and people who worked at the restaurant learned how to make it, so they knew it as well," Angie Allman says. "I think things changed when it went on the retail market. When we started to sell it commercially in 2009, we decided to keep [the Allman recipe] more of a secret, which I guess most commercial beer cheese vendors do."

"Funny story, though. We were yard sale-ing," Ian says. "I came across a little recipe box just full of recipes. I was going through it, and there was a recipe for beer cheese in the back, the same recipe we use. I'm sure they just asked for it and got it. We keep it a little closer to our chest than we used to. But it's out there."

A 1989 *Lexington Herald-Leader* article quotes Johnnie Allman: "We should've kept that cheese recipe a secret."[2] John B. says, "It was changed from time to time, but Ian and Angie always stuck with the original beer cheese recipe." After so many years, he still hasn't tired of Snappy Cheese. "I live in Florida and Ian ships me a care package every now and then, and of course I pass it out to some of my friends, too. I still love it. I've never grown tired of it."

The Allmans' story is only the beginning of beer cheese. Somewhere along the way a warm dip called "beer cheese" emerged, but it did not fork from Kentucky beer cheese and perhaps existed before the 1930s. John B. wasn't even aware that warm beer cheese existed.

John Ellison, manager of the Newport, Kentucky, franchise of German restaurant Hofbräuhaus, tells me Germany doesn't have beer cheese. "The two times I've been over there I have never seen it at a restaurant," he says. "Not even a beer hall. I would kind of guess it was an American thing." A German cheese spread called *obatzda* (soft cheeses, butter) exists, but it typically doesn't contain any beer.

The terminology is important. Throughout this book, when I write "beer cheese," I'm discussing the Kentucky-style cold spread, unless otherwise noted. On a lot of menus in Kentucky—and nationally—warmed beer cheese will be described as "beer cheese queso" or "beer cheese sauce" or "beer cheese fondue," but most places simply write "beer cheese." The dip is usually served with a warm Bavarian soft pretzel. "I always get annoyed when I go somewhere and they tell me they have beer cheese, but it's hot [in temperature]," says Zac Wright, taproom manager at Country Boy Brewing. "Beer cheese is just not supposed to be served hot." He's correct.

Not to diminish what is probably a Wisconsin creation, but warm beer cheese and Kentucky-style beer cheese are not in the same league; they lie poles apart in taste and consistency. In preparing warm beer cheese, the beer and cheeses are added separately and whisked together. Warm beer cheese congeals when it cools and forms a film on top, whereas Kentucky beer cheese is a raw, unheated food (sometimes people will heat the beer to flatten it, but that's a faux pas) with nuanced flavors like bourbon. It's basically the difference between drinking drip coffee from a machine versus pour-over coffee. But the ocher-colored warm beer cheese is everywhere—TGI Fridays, Applebee's, Outback Steakhouse, Carl's Jr., Hardee's, and your local brewpub.

That's okay, but Kentucky beer cheese—the authentic stuff—is a rarefied dish not seen much outside the confines of Central Kentucky. In writing the book, I asked several people why they think it's not available outside of Kentucky, and everyone seemed stumped. It's beer and cheese, and it's one of the best things you'll ever eat—yet most of the country is oblivious.

For instance, I was in New Orleans in 2015 and checked out the Southern Food and Beverage Museum. It had an exhibit encompassing the iconic foods and drinks of every Southern state, including Kentucky. Ale-8 soda, bourbon, and Kentucky Fried Chicken were exhibited, but the curators did not include a single blurb about beer cheese. How could Southerners ignore something that is so Kentucky? This oversight spurred me to write this book.

Kentucky is known for its rich food culture, and beer cheese is as much a part of that as bourbon and fried chicken—maybe even more so. Beer cheese is to Kentuckians like bagels are to New Yorkers, because these foods bring communities and families together. The dish is meant to be shared; it's communal. Ask many Kentucky natives, and they'll tell you beer cheese is engrained in their families. They make it every Christmas, or they serve it at their Derby parties. It's indigenous to the Commonwealth.

The beer cheese diaspora has spread to pockets of Michigan and to Austin; Charleston, South Carolina; Nashville; Chicago; and New York, but it has a long way to go to reach the West Coast and beyond. Luckily, Big Beer Cheese (i.e., a company like Kraft) hasn't swooped in and proposed manufacturing oodles of it in a factory, thus compromising the product. (But in 2016 Carl's Jr. and Hardee's introduced a Budweiser Beer Cheese Bacon Burger and Budweiser Beer Cheese Bacon Fries, using warmed-up beer cheese as a glutinous topping.) A lot of Kentuckians like the idea of beer cheese being circulated outside of Kentucky, but personally I like the idea of Central Kentucky becoming more of a beer cheese destination. Texas-style barbecue is everywhere and so is Nashville hot chicken—but to eat those foods in the states that spawned them, crafted by the natives, is more of a genuine experience. It's the same with beer cheese.

You may be thinking, "What about pimento cheese? Isn't that similar to beer cheese?" Pimento cheese is just as Southern as beer cheese but more omnipresent and faddish. In the United States, recipes for pimento cheese sandwiches started showing up in cookbooks in the 1800s, and pimento peppers started to be canned in the early 1900s. Sometimes Kentucky restaurants will engage in equal opportunity and offer both on the same menu. Coleman Magness's *Pimento Cheese: The Cookbook* features a recipe for Beer Cheese Pimento Cheese, combining two of the South's best cheese spreads. With a little push, maybe beer cheese will have the ubiquity of pimento.[3]

Whereas pimento cheese screams "the South," beer cheese symbolizes "Kentucky." Leon's Oyster Shop opened in Charleston, South Carolina, in 2014. Owner Brooks Reitz is Kentucky-born, so he placed Kentucky-style beer cheese on the menu. After a brief run, it disappeared. "We love it, but it wasn't very popular when we offered it," a restaurant representative says. If people from Charleston—one of the greatest food cities in the nation—can't accept it, what chance does beer cheese have beyond Central Kentucky? But in a state where there are more bourbon barrels than people, Kentucky will find a way to share their kick-ass beer cheese with the rest of the world.

## Beer Cheese in Cookbooks

The first mention of beer cheese in a cookbook can be traced to 1949, when Marion W. Flexner wrote about it in *Out of Kentucky Kitchens* (see p. 40). "In the days when free lunches were served in Kentucky saloons with every five-cent glass of beer, we were told of a wonderful beer cheese that decked every bar," she wrote. "Finally, we found someone who had eaten it and who told us vaguely how to prepare it." She explains the sandwich spread also "makes a perfect understudy for 'Welsh Rabbit.' [I think she meant rarebit.] But we usually put the jar of cheese on a tray, surround it with toasted crackers, and let each guest eat his fill." She explicitly says not to use processed cheese.[4] This type of "cheese" is only 51 percent real cheese, with the rest composed of emulsifiers, preservatives, artificial flavors, and salt. Processed cheese comes stored in a box or a can and has a long shelf life because a lot of varieties don't need to be refrigerated. (American cheese isn't 100 percent real cheese, but it does need to be properly stored.)

What one serves with beer cheese matters. Saltines and Ritz and Club crackers, celery and carrots, pretzels, and kettle chips are classic hand-to-mouth delivery systems. I prefer hard pretzels to soft and crackers to veggies, though celery is okay.

No two beer cheeses taste alike. Each one has a different color, from off-white to light yellow to nuclear orange. This depends on the color of the cheese base. Some people want their beer cheese to be stiff in consistency, or spreadable, whereas others prefer a creamy, dipable result that won't break a cracker or chip. (This is my personal preference, too.) With the advent of craft beer, we now have interminable options for what kind of beer to add, unlike decades ago when the choices were Budweiser or Pabst Blue Ribbon. Purists, like the makers of River Rat Beer Cheese, still prefer domestic beer. People also have access to more varieties of cheeses, especially ones that aren't labeled "cheese food," like Velveeta. You'll encounter old beer cheese recipes mostly in the appetizer sections of cookbooks compiled by women's church groups, homemaker associations, hospitals, charities, Junior Leagues, and city-specific organizations; they mostly appear in Kentucky cookbooks, not Southern ones.

Louisville's Cabbage Patch Circle's book of "famous Kentucky recipes" calls for "two pounds of good snappy cheese," minced garlic, onion, Worcestershire sauce, cayenne, Tabasco, and boiled beer. This recipe, and a lot of others, suggest grinding the cheese as opposed to grating it.[5]

*Villa Family Muncheon*, circa 1982, is a spiral-bound, typewritten, slender cookbook with a beer cheese recipe that again calls for the beer to be boiled and cooled. (However, I contend it's best to flatten the beer either by setting it out overnight or whisking some of the carbonation out of it. By releasing the gases, there will be less air in the final cheese product.) A roll of "Nippy Cheese" (a processed cheese) is required, along with Velveeta, cream cheese, Worcestershire sauce, minced onion, and garlic salt (but no cayenne). Chill the mixture overnight and serve it in a rye bread bowl. This recipe and the Cabbage Patch version catered to the ladies-who-lunch crowd, those who wanted an easy recipe to throw together for a large gathering.[6]

The inverse recipe, taken from *Berea's Best* (1978), another typed, spiral-bound cookbook, involves a spicy blend of red hot sauce, Tabasco sauce, red pepper flakes, chili powder, garlic, onion, and beer mixed with the cheese.[7]

St. Thomas Mothers Club's *40th Anniversary Edition Cookbook* (1981) offers up a warm and mild beer cheese recipe served in a bread bowl. It also promotes Kraft Nippy Cheese, warmed-up beer, and "oleo" (an abbreviation for oleomargarine).[8]

A side note for vegetarians: a lot of beer cheese recipes call for the addition of Worcestershire sauce (which contains anchovies). Because a lot of recipes are secret, it's best to ask the cook if there's Worcestershire sauce in it. Another concern for vegetarians: a lot of cheeses contain rennet—a starter enzyme that's created in the stomach lining of a calf. Beer cheese ingredients do not list whether the cheese used has rennet or not, so just to be cautious, visit your local market and purchase cheese that reads "microbial rennet" or "vegetarian rennet" on the label, and make it yourself.

Beer cheese recipes appear in a few Kentucky Derby–themed cookbooks: *Derby Entertaining* (2000), which calls for grated Cracker Barrel cheese; *Derby*

*Museum Cookbook* (1986), made with finely ground sharp and mild cheddar; and *Derby Start to Finish* (2011), which features extra sharp cheddar and blue cheese). *Beechwood Cooks* (no date) uses Roquefort blue cheese and Kraft Nippy Cheese.[9]

New York State sharp cheddar, olives, and hot peppers highlight one of the more unusual recipes, this one from *Capital Kitchens*, a 1974 cookbook compiled by the Frankfort Younger Women's Club. This is the only recipe I saw in which olives are blended into the cheese.[10]

Richard T. Hougen—who ran the Boone Tavern in Berea—lists a recipe for Snappy Cheese Spread in his cookbook *Look No Further* (1951). Hougen's version combines cheddar, cream cheese, ketchup, butter, paprika, dry mustard, and—oddly—chicken broth.[11]

The recipe book from the *Children's Home of Northern Kentucky* (2002) evidences how later on more *umami* flavors were integrated into beer cheese. Velveeta (the recipe doesn't say whether to melt it or not), sharp cheddar, garlic powder, horseradish mustard, onion flakes, beer, hot sauce, soy sauce, Worcestershire, and chopped jalapeños are blended and served in a rye bread bowl.[12]

Tomato bases circulate in two cookbook recipes. *Kentucky Tale Gating* (2004) uses tomato paste.[13] *The Lee Bros. Charleston Kitchen* (2013) includes a recipe from an old Charleston, South Carolina, restaurant named Henry's. The cheese spread recipe isn't even referred to as beer cheese—it's named Henry's Cheese Spread—but the recipe clearly states to add sharp cheddar, beer, lemon juice, and ketchup. Other recipes outside of Kentucky also don't always call the spread beer cheese. I've seen it labeled "cheddar with beer" spread, which is not exactly the same thing.[14]

Elizabeth Ross assembles a whopping thirteen beer cheese recipes in her collection *Kentucky Keepsakes* (1996). Colonel George M. Chinn's Beer Cheese calls for longhorn cheese (round Colby cheese), garlic, yellow peppers, Frank's RedHot sauce, and stale beer. "Blend the garlic, peppers, beer, hot sauce in a blender," the recipe says. "Blend cheese and liquid mixture in an electric mixer. Serve with crackers and a soothing, nonflammable drink." The two-step preparation seems like more work than is necessary (but the drink idea sounds good). *Kentucky Keepsakes* includes a beer cheese recipe reprinted from *The Civil Wah Cookbook from Boogar Hollow* (1972), which is one of the few versions featured in a Southern cookbook. Yet another recipe, this from Madonna Smith Echols's *The Crowning Recipes of Kentucky,* blends Swiss cheese with the cheddar cheese. Three Snappy Cheese recipes emerge, including the Jim Curry's Men's Bar recipe made with rat cheese (a processed cheese), beer, sharp cheese, onions, garlic, red pepper, and dehydrated horseradish. A recipe called Quantity Cheese Spread asks for Accent salt (a flavor

> ### Beer Cheese Baked Potatoes and Fries
> Melt a few tablespoons of beer cheese into baked potato skins, or drizzle melted beer cheese on fries. You can also use cold beer cheese as a fry dipping sauce.

enhancer with MSG) and Lawry's seasoning (but I guarantee adding them will lower the quality of the taste). Finally, Ross reprints what is supposedly the original Allman's recipe: 2½ pounds of Ye Olde Tavern Cheese (a semisoft cheese), 4 ounces stale beer, 1½ teaspoons granulated garlic, and ½ teaspoon of cayenne. A Google search for Ye Olde Tavern leads to Old Tavern Club Cheese, based in Waukesha, Wisconsin. They've been in business for more than ninety years and could conceivably be the place where the Allmans have sourced their cold-pack cheddar for decades. Have we unspooled the mystery? Who knows?[15]

By studying the trajectory of beer cheese recipes in cookbooks from the 1950s to the present, I found that the recipes evolved from homey versions offered up by women's clubs and charities to sophisticated adaptations in chef-driven books. Chef Jonathan Lundy's 2009 cookbook *Jonathan's Bluegrass Table* contains a recipe for a beer cheese made with beer, bourbon, and caramelized onions.[16] A recipe for beer cheese hummus (see p. 45) appears in Maggie Green's *The Kentucky Fresh Cookbook* (2011), and a few Kentucky chefs reveal their beer cheese recipes in Green's *Tasting Kentucky: Favorite Recipes from the Bluegrass State* (2016).[17] Nashville has an emerging beer cheese scene, and in Jennifer Justus's cookbook *Nashville Eats*, she supplies a recipe for Bloomy Rind Beer Cheese using four-year-old Hook's Wisconsin sharp cheddar, microplane-grated garlic, and beer from a Nashville brewery.[18] In the future, we'll probably see more of these epicurean recipes represented in Southern cookbooks.

## Notes

1. Kentucky Legislature, www.lrc.ky.gov/record/13rs/HB54.htm.

2. Don Edwards, "Restaurateur Reveled in Laughter, Life on the Kentucky River," *Lexington Herald-Leader*, Nov. 1, 1989.

3. Perre Coleman Magness, *Pimento Cheese: The Cookbook* (New York: St. Martin's Griffin, 2014), 2–4.

4. Marion W. Flexner, *Out of Kentucky Kitchens* (Lexington: University of Kentucky Press, 1949, rpt. 2010), 30.

5. Cabbage Patch Circle, *Cabbage Patch Famous Kentucky Recipes* (Louisville: The Circle, 1952), 13.

6. Ami Beckman, *Villa Family Muncheon* (n.p., 1982), 2.

7. Younger Woman's Club, *Berea's Best* (Berea, KY: Younger Woman's Club, 1968), 116.

8. *The 40th Anniversary Edition Cookbook: St. Thomas Mothers Club* (Fort Thomas, KY: Cookbook Publishing Inc, 1981), 11.

9. Paula Cunningham, Michelle Stone, and Verne Dobbs, eds., *Derby Entertaining: Traditional Kentucky* (Kuttawa, KY: McClanahan Publishing, 2000), 9; *Kentucky Derby Museum Cookbook* (Louisville: Kentucky Derby Museum, 1986), 23; Sarah Fritschner, *Derby: Start to Finish* (Louisville: Butler Books, 2011), 55; *Beechwood Cooks* (Fort Mitchell, KY: Beechwood School, n.d.), 6.

10. Frankfort Younger Women's Club, *Capital Kitchens*, 2nd ed. (Frankfort, KY: The Club, 1974), 2.

11. Richard T. Hougen, *Look No Further* (Nashville: Parthenon Press, 1951), 20.

12. Susan Kettles, ed., *Children's Home of Northern Kentucky: Recipe Book* (Covington: Children's Home of Northern Kentucky), 9.

13. Kelli Oakley and Jayna Oakley, *Kentucky Tale Gating: Stories with Sauce* (Lexington, KY: Oakley Press, 2004), 33.

14. Matt and Ted Lee, *The Lee Bros. Charleston Kitchen* (New York: Clarkson Potter, 2013), 47.

15. Elizabeth Ross, *Kentucky Keepsakes* (Kuttawa, KY: McClanahan Publishing, 1996), 33–38.

16. Jonathan Lundy, *Jonathan's Bluegrass Table: Redefining Kentucky Cuisine* (Louisville: Butler Books, 2009), 85.

17. Maggie Green, *The Kentucky Fresh Cookbook* (Lexington: University Press of Kentucky, 2011), 52; Maggie Green, *Tasting Kentucky: Favorite Recipes from the Bluegrass State* (Helena, MT: Farcountry Press, 2016), 37, 41, 95–96.

18. Jennifer Justus, *Nashville Eats: Hot Chicken, Buttermilk Biscuits, and 100 More Recipes from Music City* (New York: Stewart, Tabori, & Chang, 2015), 41.

# 2

# RECIPES

*Unless otherwise noted, the beer is understood to be flattened at room temperature before adding it to the cheese. (See the sidebar on page 41 for beer-flattening instructions.)*

## Beer Cheese and Mushroom Risotto

*Serves 4*

4 cups vegetable broth (or chicken broth)

1 tablespoon olive oil

1 shallot, diced

1 garlic clove, minced

1 cup mushrooms, diced

1½ cups arborio rice

½ cup beer (hoppy), not flattened
5 ounces beer cheese

Pour the broth into a saucepan and bring to a simmer over medium heat. Add the olive oil to an iron skillet and sauté the shallot and garlic over medium heat until soft. Lower heat to a simmer. Add the mushrooms and cook for 2 more minutes. Add in the rice and a cup of broth and stir so the rice absorbs the broth. The mixture may look soupy, but the extra liquid will evaporate. After 5 minutes, continue adding the broth in portions until it's gone, stirring constantly. This process will take 15–20 minutes. Stir in the beer last. Once all the broth is absorbed, mix in the beer cheese until it melts into the risotto. Serve immediately.

## Beer Cheese Nugget Bites

*Makes about 2 dozen bites*

1½ cups tepid water (105°F to 110°F)
1 (¼-ounce) packet active dry yeast (2 ¼ teaspoons)
2½ cups flour
1 teaspoon salt

1 tablespoon olive oil

4 ounces beer cheese, room temperature

2 cups water

2 tablespoons baking soda

6 tablespoons butter, melted

Coarse sea salt (optional)

Preheat oven to 400°F.

Dissolve the yeast into the tepid water. Wait 5 minutes, until the yeast starts to bubble. In the meantime, mix the flour and salt in a separate bowl. Use a spoon to stir the dissolved yeast mixture into the flour and salt. The dry ingredients should be completely incorporated to make a dough. Knead the dough for a few minutes until it's stretchable and not sticky. Place it in an oiled bowl and let rise for 30 minutes in a warm (but not hot) place. It will puff up a bit.

Place the dough on a floured surface. Pull it into 12-inch-long ropes (at least an inch in diameter) and cut into 1-inch or ½-inch-long pieces. The smaller the better. Flatten out the cut dough pieces by hand and add about 1 teaspoon of beer cheese to the center of each. Press down on the beer cheese to spread it. Gently fold the sides of the pieces together, using a dab of water to seal the edges so the beer cheese won't ooze out during baking.

Pour 2 cups of water into a saucepan and bring to boil. Dissolve the baking soda into it then reduce to a simmer. Add the dough pieces one at a time (in batches of no more than 5) and let them bathe for about a minute, turning them over once. Remove from the water and place on a baking sheet lined with parchment paper or a silicone baking mat. Make sure the nuggets are spaced apart and not touching each other. Brush the tops with melted butter. Sprinkle with sea salt, if you like.

Bake the nuggets about 15–20 minutes, flipping them over after 10 minutes. Some of the cheese may ooze out.

## Beer Cheese Buttermilk Biscuits

*Buttermilk biscuits are a Southern staple, and inserting beer cheese gives them a cheese straw flavor. Serve these as a breakfast sandwich, as a side entrée, or as a snack.*

### Makes about 12 biscuits

2 cups flour
1 tablespoon baking powder
12 tablespoons (1½ sticks) cold, unsalted butter, diced

Beer cheese
buttermilk biscuits.
(Photo by the author)

½ cup cold buttermilk, shaken

2 eggs, one reserved for egg wash

4 ounces beer cheese, room temperature

1 tablespoon water

Preheat oven to 425°F.

Put the flour and baking powder in the bowl of a stand mixer fitted with dough hooks. With the mixer set on low, add in the butter and mix until the butter is broken up into little balls.

Whisk the buttermilk, whole egg, and beer cheese in a measuring cup.

Add it to the flour and butter mixture, still mixing on low speed. Once mixed together, remove the dough from the bowl and knead it on a floured board. Roll the dough out into a 10 x 5-inch rectangle. The dough should be around ½-inch thick. With a sharp, floured knife, cut the dough lengthwise in half and then across in quarters, making 8 rough rectangles.

Separate the second egg, place the white in a small dish, and add the water to make an egg wash.

Arrange the rectangles on a baking sheet and brush the tops with the egg wash. Cook for 20–25 minutes, or until brown and somewhat puffy.

## Crab Broccoli and Beer Cheese Casserole

*When I was growing up, my mom made broccoli and cheese casserole for the family, but I've updated it by adding beer cheese. Along with the broccoli, you can also add kale and other veggies.*

### Serves 4

1 bunch fresh broccoli, chopped (about a pound, crowns and stems)
2 tablespoons olive oil
2 tablespoons onion, diced
½ teaspoon salt

2 tablespoons flour

4 ounces beer cheese

1 tablespoon lemon juice

½ pound lump crab meat

Preheat oven 350°F.

Bring the water to a boil and then lower to medium heat. Add the chopped broccoli pieces and cook until just tender, about 5 minutes. Drain the semi cooked broccoli and place it in an 8 x 11-inch baking dish.

Add the olive oil to a saucepan and heat on medium. Sauté the diced onion and then stir in the salt and flour. Gradually add dollops of beer cheese, stirring constantly. Cook over low heat until thickened. Stir in the lemon juice. Mix in the crab meat and pour the mixture over the broccoli.

Bake for 30 minutes, or until the broccoli gets crispy.

## Garin's Beer Cheese

*I experimented with different cheeses and beer and came up with this recipe. Crushed mustard seeds add the right amount of heat. I went for a smoked cheddar, and the coffee stout adds a richness to it—and also*

*more beer. This beer cheese works well in the risotto recipe (page 23).*
*In addition to beer, nothing says Kentucky like bourbon.*

### Makes about 3 cups

> 1 pound smoked cheddar cheese
> ¼ pound Lakefront Brewery beer cheese coffee stout cheese, from
>     Wisconsin Cheese Market
> 2 tablespoons mustard seeds, brown and/or yellow, crushed
> 1 shallot, minced
> 1 garlic clove, peeled
> ½ cup hoppy beer
> 1 tablespoon bourbon

Note: If you can't find the Lakefront beer cheese or another type of beer-washed cheese, then substitute gouda and add 2 tablespoons of flattened coffee stout beer. Shred the cheeses and add to the work bowl of a food processor. Use a mortar and pestle to grind the mustard seeds semifine. Add the shallots, garlic clove, and mustard seeds to the cheese and blend. Slowly add in the beer, followed by the bourbon. Scrape down the sides of the processor with a spatula to incorporate any sticky bits. Blend until smooth and creamy.

Handful microgreens, not chopped

1 ounce pickled vegetables

½ pound ground bison or steak, cooked and drained (optional)

2 tablespoons crème fraîche or plain yogurt, for topping

Add the beans to three cups of water and hard boil them for 5 minutes, then cover and simmer until cooked (at least 30 minutes).

### To Make the Beer Cheese Mornay

Add room-temperature beer cheese to a saucepan and warm to medium heat. Add the milk (or half-and-half) to thin it, stirring constantly to make a sauce, then remove from the heat. In another saucepan, melt butter and whisk in flour to make a roux. Stir until the mixture turns slightly brown. Add in the beer cheese sauce and mix well.

### To Make the Nachos

Place a layer of tortilla chips on a plate and pour half of the beer cheese sauce over the chips, making sure to coat every one. Heap the cooked beans, salsa, diced peppers, cilantro, microgreens, pickled veggies, and meat on the nachos. Top with the rest of the sauce. Finish with a scoop of crème fraîche or yogurt set in the middle of the nachos.

# Beer Cheese Bagels

### *Makes about 12 bagels*

> 1½ cups tepid water (105°F to 110°F)
>
> 1 (¼-ounce) packet active dry yeast (2¼ teaspoons)
>
> 7 ¾ cups King Arthur bread flour, plus 2 tablespoons for flour surface
>
> 2 tablespoons local honey or malt syrup
>
> 1 teaspoon kosher salt
>
> 5 ounces beer cheese
>
> ½ tablespoon olive oil
>
> 2 quarts water

Dissolve the yeast and 4 cups of flour into a bowl of tepid water and set aside at room temperature for two hours so it can ferment. Add the yeast mixture (i.e., the "sponge") along with the rest of the flour, honey (or malt syrup), salt, and beer cheese to the bowl of a stand mixer fitted with dough hooks. Mix on low. Slowly increase the speed and mix until the dough is elastic and not sticky. If it's still sticky, add more flour. Scrape down the sides of the bowl to make sure everything is well blended.

Form the dough into a ball. Place the dough on a floured surface. Shape it into about a dozen 8-inch ropes and form each into a circle. Use a dab of water to stick the ends together. Brush with olive oil. Place the bagels on a baking sheet, cover with plastic wrap, and refrigerate at least overnight.

Preheat the oven to 425°F.

Take the bagels out of the fridge. Fill an 8-quart pot with water, bring it to a boil, and then reduce it to a simmer. Drop the bagels, one at a time, into the stovetop bath. Allow them to bathe for 30 seconds, turning over once. Line a baking sheet with parchment paper or use a silicone baking mat. Use tongs to remove bagels from the water and place them on the baking sheet. Make sure the bagels do not touch.

Bake the bagels until they start to turn golden brown. Remove from the oven and use a butter knife to smear room-temperature beer cheese on them. Return them to the oven for another few minutes, or until the beer cheese starts to bubble and brown.

Remove from oven and cool.

## Beer Cheese Cheese Ball

*When I did research for this book, I leafed through a lot of old Kentucky cookbooks and most of them had at least one recipe for a cheese ball. Some recipes integrated pineapple into the ball, and others added salmon or corned beef. Yet none of the recipes had beer cheese in them. I thought, why not? Plus, it's fun to say "beer cheese cheese ball."*

*Makes 1 6-inch ball*

8 ounces cream cheese
4 ounces beer cheese
¼ cup parsley, chopped
1 tablespoon onion, minced
½ cup pretzels, ground

Note: In place of pretzels, you can grind up Ritz crackers or pecans and coat the ball with them.

Allow the cream cheese and beer cheese to come to room temperature. Mix the two in a bowl. Add the parsley and onion and stir until well blended.

A beer cheese cheese ball. (Photo by the author)

Shape the mixture into a ball using either your hands or a spatula. Chill the ball in the refrigerator for a few hours.

Place the pretzels in a food processor and grind them for 30 seconds, or until fine.

Immediately before serving, take the beer cheese ball out of the fridge. Spread the ground pretzels on a plate and roll and sprinkle the pretzels on the ball until it's coated. Serve with crackers.

# Wrecking Bar Brewpub's Kale Ale Fondue

*Chef Terry Koval of the Atlanta gastropub Wrecking Bar incorporates kale into his warm beer cheese fondue, making it slightly healthy. You can cut this recipe down.*

### *Makes 2 quarts*

¼ pound butter (4 ounces, or 1 stick)

½ cup unbleached all-purpose flour

1¼ cups heavy cream

2½ cups milk

2 tablespoons kosher salt

1 tablespoon dry Colman's Mustard

1½ ounces Worcestershire sauce

1½ cups pimentos, diced

½ pound sharp Wisconsin cheddar, grated

½ pound 24-year aged Beemster gouda, grated

1 cup IPA beer

1 to 1½ quart raw kale, chopped (1 large bunch)

½ tablespoon smoked paprika

In a large saucepan, heat the butter over medium-high heat. Add the flour all at once, whisking vigorously. Cook, stirring constantly, until you smell a toasty aroma and the flour and butter are fully combined.

Slowly whisk in the heavy cream and milk. Add the salt, mustard, Worcestershire, and pimentos. Cook this at a slow simmer for 15 minutes, allowing the liquid to thicken while whisking occasionally.

Slowly add the grated cheeses, whisking constantly as you bring the fondue to a simmer. Then slowly whisk in your IPA of choice. Bring the fondue back up to a simmer.

Add the raw kale, and dust with smoked paprika.

Serve with soft pretzels and your favorite local raw veggies.

## Gralehaus Beer Cheese

*Chef Andy Myers of Louisville's Gralehaus provides his beer cheese recipe, which is inspired by the neighboring Holy Grale. The key is to let the food processor run for at least 10 minutes to create a glossy beer cheese.*

### Makes about 2½ cups

⅛ cup (2 tablespoons) buttermilk

1 garlic clove, minced

2 teaspoons Crystal hot sauce

5 ounces cream cheese

3 ounces hoppy beer

6 ounces aged white cheddar, grated

1 teaspoon of chopped fresh chives, for topping

Blend the buttermilk, garlic, hot sauce, and cream cheese in a food processor for 30 seconds.

While the food processor is running, add the beer and the cheddar, alternating between approximately 1 ounce of beer and approximately 2 ounces of shredded cheddar until it is all incorporated. Once it is all added, let the food processor run for an additional 5–8 minutes, or until the mixture is completely smooth. You should not be able to see any small bits of cheddar. The beer cheese should be one homogeneous spread. Garnish with chives to serve.

## Marion W. Flexner's Beer Cheese Recipe

*The earliest beer cheese recipe that I found in a cookbook was in Flexner's* Out of Kentucky Kitchens, *published in 1949.*

## How to Flatten Beer

I've tried three different methods to decarbonate or flatten the beer prior to blending it with the cheese.

The easiest method (but most time-consuming) involves pouring the beer into a bowl and leaving it on the kitchen countertop overnight, typically six to eight hours. This is the most organic way to flatten it and the method I recommend.

But if you're pressed for time, you can pour the beer in a microwave-safe bowl and nuke it for one minute. I don't like heating up the beer—it doesn't taste as good—but it's a quick method. You also can simmer the beer on the stovetop for a couple of minutes.

The third method involves a little elbow grease. Pour the beer into a mixer-sized bowl. Using a whisk, beat the beer continuously for 5 minutes. The beer will foam, but the remaining liquid will lose carbonation. This is also a good way to get some exercise.

1 pound aged cheddar cheese (sharp)

1 pound American or "rat" cheese (bland)

2 or 3 garlic pods (to taste), sectioned and peeled

3 tablespoons Worcestershire sauce

1 teaspoon salt

1 teaspoon powered mustard

Dash of Tabasco sauce or cayenne pepper

¾ of a 12-ounce bottle of beer (about 1 cup or less)

Grind the cheese (do not use processed cheese) with the garlic pods. (Since the recipe is from the 1940s, Marion probably did this by hand, but you can use a food processor or blender to save elbow grease.) Mix in the Worcestershire sauce, salt, mustard, and Tabasco or cayenne. Add the cheese mixture to the bowl of an electric mixer set on low speed; slowly add enough beer to make a paste smooth enough to spread. Store in covered jars and keep refrigerated until needed.

## Bouquet Beer Cheese

*Bouquet Restaurant and Wine Bar is an award-winning farm-to-table restaurant located in the MainStrasse neighborhood of Covington, Kentucky, across the Ohio River from Cincinnati. Chef Stephen Williams doesn't have beer cheese on his menu, so I asked him to come up with a recipe for the book. He uses mainly Kentucky ingredients, including*

*Kentucky cheese and a beer from a local brewery called Braxton Brew-ery. He also includes his recipes for house-made mustard and smoked hot sauce. (bouquetrestaurant.com)*

### Makes about 3 cups

### To Make the Bouquet Smoked Hot Sauce

½ medium red onion, chopped
1 tablespoon olive oil
4 pounds dried chilies
1 tablespoon fennel seeds
1 tablespoon cumin seeds
1 tablespoon coriander seeds
1 tablespoon garlic confit (garlic cloves poached in olive oil)
5 strips lemon zest
3 cups apple cider vinegar
3½ cups white vinegar

Note: If you don't want to make your own hot sauce or mustard, substitute a premade mustard and hot sauce you like. But if you do make an entire batch, you can store it in the fridge for weeks to use with other recipes.

Sweat the onions in olive oil over medium heat until the liquid is evaporated. Make sure the onions don't brown. Add them to a food processor, then combine the dried chilies, fennel, cumin, coriander, garlic, lemon zest, and vinegars and blend them together.

### *To Make the Bouquet Mustard*

> 5 ounces water
> 10 tablespoons yellow mustard seeds
> 2½ tablespoons black/brown mustard seeds
> 2 ounces oil
> 3 tablespoons ground turmeric
> 2 tablespoons salt
> 4 ounces maple syrup or 3½ ounces honey
> ¼ teaspoon cayenne pepper
> 17½ ounces rice wine vinegar

Boil the water and add the mustard seeds. Remove from the heat and let sit for 20 minutes.

Drain and agitate the seeds in a strainer, and then put them in a blender.

Add the turmeric, salt, maple syrup (or honey), and cayenne to the blender and mix on low speed. Slowly add in the vinegar to emulsify.

### *To Make the Beer Cheese*

1 pound Kenny's Farmhouse white cheddar, grated
1 tablespoon garlic, minced
1 cup Braxton Storm Cream Ale
1 tablespoon Bouquet mustard
½ teaspoon Bouquet smoked hot sauce
1 teaspoon of Worcestershire sauce
Salt and pepper to taste

Shred the cheese on a box grater, and whisk the carbonation out of the beer. Add the shredded cheese, garlic, beer, mustard, hot sauce, and Worcestershire sauce to a food processor. Blend until smooth. Season with salt and pepper.

## Beer Cheese Hummus

*In Maggie Green's* The Kentucky Fresh Cookbook, *she writes, "This hummus is a dairy-free alternative with the same snappy flavor."*

*Though the recipe has "cheese" in its title, no cheese is used, not even vegan cheese. Vegan cheese isn't advised, as it doesn't blend well.*

### Makes about 2½ cups

1½ cups cooked (or one 15-ounce can) chickpeas, drained

½ cup roasted pepper strips

½ cup beer

¼ cup tahini

2 cloves garlic, minced

Juice of 1 lemon

2 tablespoons olive oil

½ teaspoon salt

¼ teaspoon cayenne pepper

Place all the ingredients in a blender or food processor and blend or process until the mixture is smooth. Refrigerate for at least 1 hour for the best flavor.

# Sunrise Bakery Baguette Chips

*Steven Francis Matherly owns Lexington's Sunrise Bakery. His crunchy baguette chips are served with Olivia's Beer Cheese's at the West Sixth Brewery Greenroom, next door to the bakery, and also at West Sixth's main brewery.*

Note: If you're too busy to make your own baguette, purchase the bread from your local bakery and skip ahead to the chips part.

## *To Make the Baguette*

### *Makes one 26-inch baguette*

2 cups tepid water (105°F to 110°F)
½ ounce active yeast
3⅓ cups bread flour, high protein (Bob's Red Mill is a good choice.)
3 teaspoons salt

Preheat the oven 450°F.

Place yeast in a bowl and add tepid water and mix. Let sit for 5 minutes. Add the yeast mixture and flour to a stand-mixer bowl equipped with dough hooks. Mix for 10 minutes. Add the salt and mix for 5 more minutes. When finished, place the dough in another bowl or container and cover with a lid or towel. Let it sit for at least 1 hour in a warm spot.

Weigh out 2 or 3 14-ounce pieces. Round each into a ball and let sit covered for 10–20 minutes.

Grab a ball and smack it down onto a floured surface. Grab it lengthwise and roll it up. It should be around a foot long. (Repeat with the other pieces of dough.)

Let the loaf sit for 10–20 more minutes. Then, starting in the middle, roll outward with both hands, back and forth, finishing the ends in a nice tip. The loaf should be around 26 inches long. Let it sit for 10–20 minutes more, and then place it onto a wooden peel to transfer it to an oven stone, or bake the loaf on a sheet tray. Make 4 slashes down the length with a knife or razor and load the loaf into the oven 20–28 minutes.

To better fit the baguette into small ovens, you can cut it into two 13-inch loafs.

### To Make the Chips

1 baguette
¼ cup extra virgin olive oil

1 teaspoon course sea salt

1 teaspoon pepper

1 tablespoon dried oregano

Preheat oven to 400°F.

Slice the baguette into discs around ¼-inch thick. Lay the discs out on sheet tray and drizzle extra virgin olive oil generously all over the pieces. Season with sea salt, black pepper, and dried oregano, and bake 8–12 minutes.

## Pawpaw Beer Cheese

*Sara Bir is a home cook, a freelance food writer, and the author of* The Pocket Pawpaw Cookbook *(sausagetarian.com). Based in Marietta, Ohio, she's also a bit of a pawpaw fruit expert. For this book, she melded pawpaws and beer cheese together into something fantastic. "Pawpaws are a tropical-tasting tree fruit native to North America and can be found growing wild quite abundantly in woods across Kentucky," she says. "Kentucky State University (KSU) Land Grant Program has the only full-time pawpaw research program in the world. So marrying beer cheese and pawpaw, two very Kentuckian foods, is a natural move. The pawpaw won't be the first flavor to strike the palate, but its funky-bright character works very well with the cheese here. To get extra crazy, use a pawpaw beer, or just serve one on the side." Jackie O's in Athens, Ohio, brews a delicious seasonal pawpaw beer. Albany, Ohio, a few miles outside of Athens, hosts the Ohio Pawpaw Festival every September.*

*Pawpaws are usually in season from September through mid-October, but you can mail-order frozen Pawpaw Pleasures year-round through Earthy Delights (earthy.com).*

### Makes about 2½ cups

12 ounces extra sharp orange cheddar cheese, grated
About 3 fluid ounces (⅓ cup plus 2 tablespoons) skinless, seedless pawpaw
    pulp
2 teaspoons dry ground mustard powder
2 cloves garlic, smashed
1–2 teaspoons red pepper sauce
⅓ cup pale ale, plus a tablespoon or two more if needed

Grate the cheese. Put it into the work bowl of a food processor fitted with a steel blade. Add the pawpaw, mustard, garlic, and pepper sauce. Turn on the

## Beer Cheese Grits

Purchase your grits from Weisenberger Mill (weisenberger.com) in Midway, Kentucky; from Louisville's Louismill (louismill.com); or from Shagbark Mill (shagbarkmill.com) in Athens, Ohio. Add three cups of water to a saucepan to one cup of grits. Boil at medium high heat, then turn down to let the grits simmer for 20 minutes, covered. The water should evaporate. While waiting for the grits to cook, slice up spring onions and lightly char them in a frying pan or skillet. Mix a few ounces of beer cheese into the grits, and then add the onions. Serve warm.

Another option is to spread the beer cheese grits in a baking pan and refrigerate until they are firm. Cut the cooled grits into squares. Add a whisked raw egg to one dish and a cup of panko to another. Dip the grits squares first in the panko, then the egg, and then the panko again. Fry the dredged grits in olive oil until they're crispy.

processor and slowly pour the beer through the feed tube. If the beer cheese is too stiff, add more pawpaw or beer, one tablespoon at a time. You're aiming for a consistency that's spreadable but not runny.

Taste the beer cheese, preferably on a cracker or a carrot stick. Add more pepper sauce if you need it to be snappier. This beer cheese will mellow over time. Tightly covered and refrigerated, it should keep for 1 to 2 weeks.

Notes: I like my beer cheese a little on the stiffer side (more spreadable than dipable). I also noticed this version got a little stiffer after it had been in the fridge a few days.

Pawpaws oxidize like crazy, and after 2–3 days, some subtle brown areas appeared in the beer cheese. This is just the pawpaw asserting itself—it does that, even with the acid from the beer. It's not an indication that the beer cheese has gone bad. As it sits, the pawpaw aroma will become a little stronger, too.

## Beer Cheese Cupcakes with Beer Cheese Buttercream

*I also asked Sara Bir to develop a beer cheese cupcake recipe, and this is what she came up with. She realized using premade beer cheese worked better than adding the beer and cheese separately. "I think the flavor of beer cheese is different from just beer and cheese—there are other ingredients, first of all, and secondly, there's that melding and mellowing of flavor that happens to make a new flavor," she says. "But I found that too much beer cheese in the batter or buttercream made end products that didn't set right, so I had to keep the beer cheese ratio lower than I'd have liked."*

Beer cheese and cupcakes,
together at last.
Baked by Sara Bir.
(Courtesy Sara Bir)

*(Author's note: The result is a sweet and savory dessert, almost like a muffin. Even those who aren't a fan of desserts will like this one. The recipe may seem daunting, but it's easy to make and it's a game-changer for parties and luncheons.)*

***Makes 12 cupcakes***

## *For the Cupcakes*

> 2 cups all-purpose flour
>
> 2 teaspoons baking powder
>
> ¼ teaspoon salt
>
> ¼ teaspoon ground mustard powder
>
> ½ cup pale ale or brown ale (I used Fat Tire, but any not-too-hoppy ale should do.)
>
> 1½ teaspoons vanilla extract
>
> 2 tablespoons honey
>
> 4 tablespoons (½ stick) unsalted butter, room temperature
>
> ⅓ cup stiff beer cheese, room temperature
>
> 1 cup granulated sugar
>
> 2 large eggs, room temperature

Preheat the oven to 350°F and position a rack in the center.

In a medium bowl, whisk together the flour, baking powder, salt, and mustard powder. Set aside.

In a glass measuring cup, combine the ale, vanilla, and honey. Stir to dissolve the honey. Set aside.

In the bowl of an electric mixer, combine the butter and beer cheese. Beat with the paddle attachment until well blended. Add the sugar and beat until creamy. (The mixture may not get fluffy, but don't fret.) Add the eggs one at a time, scraping the bowl with a rubber spatula after each addition.

Add half of the flour mixture to the beer cheese batter and beat until it's incorporated. With the mixer running, add half the ale mixture. Scrape down the bowl and repeat with the remaining dry and wet ingredients, ending with the ale.

Grease the rims of 12 standard-sized cupcake tins and line with paper liners. Divide the batter between the tins, filling no more than ⅔ full. (If you have any extra batter, you can bake it in a greased custard cup or ramekin.)

Bake until a toothpick inserted in the center of a cupcake comes out clean, 20–25 minutes. Cool completely on a wire rack.

## *For the Buttercream Frosting and Garnish*

8 ounces cream cheese, softened

2 tablespoons unsalted butter, softened

¼ cup stiff beer cheese, softened (the kind that's more for spreading, not for dipping)

4 cups unsifted powdered sugar

1 teaspoon vanilla extract

Thin salted pretzels, broken into pieces, for garnish

Combine the cream cheese, butter, and beer cheese in the bowl of an electric mixer. Beat until creamy. Add the powdered sugar a cup at a time, scraping down the sides of the bowl from time to time with a rubber spatula. Beat in the vanilla. The buttercream will likely be a little soft; cover it and put it in the refrigerator for an hour or so to let it set.

This buttercream is easier to pipe (squirt from a bag) than spread with a spatula. Spoon the buttercream into a pastry bag fitted with a wide star tip and pipe it onto the tops of the cooled cupcakes. (If you don't have a piping bag, spoon the buttercream into a gallon zip-top bag and snip off a quarter-inch of the corner.) As you pipe, your hands will make the buttercream warmer, so just pop the bag back in the fridge if the buttercream starts getting runny. You can use a spatula, too, as long as the buttercream stays cold. Store the frosted cupcakes in the refrigerator.

Before serving, press crushed pretzels into the buttercream for garnish.

Note: Any unused buttercream is great for dipping pretzels. You can also spread it between graham crackers to make "sandwiches" to freeze.

## Woody's Sports Bar and Grill Beer Cheese

*Stacy Lisle, owner of Woody's in Winchester, provides his spicy beer cheese recipe. Check it out on the Beer Cheese Trail (chapter 3).*

1 tablespoon cayenne

1 tablespoon fresh garlic, minced

1 tablespoon red pepper flakes

1 pound sharp cold-pack cheddar

1 pound Velveeta, room temperature

1 tablespoon Worcestershire sauce

¾ bottle (8 ounces) Miller Lite

Add all the ingredients but the beer to the work bowl of a food processor and start blending. Add the beer gradually until the mixture is smooth.

## Smoke Daddy's Smoked Jalapeño Beer Cheese

*Chef Lamar Moore shares his smoked jalapeño recipe from Chicago barbecue restaurant Smoke Daddy (see chapter 5).*

*Makes about 6 cups*

    1 pound Wisconsin sharp cheddar cheese, grated

    ½ cup Parmigiano-Reggiano cheese, finely grated

    1¾ cups mayo (My preference is Duke's.)

    3 ounces pale ale

    ¼ cup red pepper, diced into ¼ x ¼-inch pieces

    ¼ cup scallions, tops and bottoms, sliced ⅛-inch thick

    1¼ tablespoons chipotle peppers, pureed

    ¼ cup pickled jalapeño, diced into ¼ x ¼-inch pieces

    2 fresh jalapeños, seeded and diced, smoked for 1 hour

Note for smoking the jalapeños: If you don't have access to a smoker, you can use a pan with holes in it, such as an insert for steaming vegetables. Buy smoking chips (found alongside the charcoal in most grocery stores) and add enough to cover the bottom of the pan. Place the jalapeños on top of the chips, cover the pan with foil, and smoke an hour on the grill at 225°F. Be careful!

In a large bowl, mix together the first four ingredients: sharp cheddar, Parmigiano-Reggiano, mayo, and beer.

Run the cheese mixture through a meat grinder, using medium-high speed and a small grinding plate. It will look a bit like runny hamburger.

In separate bowl, combine remaining items: red peppers, scallions, chipotle peppers, and pickled and smoked jalapeños.

Combine the cheese mixture with the spicy ingredients, mixing by hand. Store cold.

Note: If you don't have a meat grinder, buy cheddar in feathered shreds instead to get the right consistency. You can also use a food processor.

## Smithtown Seafood West Sixth Porter Beer Cheese

*This recipe by Smithtown's chef, Jon Sanning, includes a rich porter. The restaurant serves this beer cheese with fresh seasonal vegetables (see chapter 5).*

### Makes about 5 cups

2 large garlic cloves, chopped
¼ medium yellow onion, chopped
1 tablespoon Crystal hot sauce (no substitutions!)
½ teaspoon Lea & Perrins Worcestershire Sauce

¼ teaspoon ground black pepper

¼ teaspoon kosher salt

½ teaspoon cayenne pepper

½ teaspoon mustard powder

1 pound and 2 ounces sharp white cheddar, grated

1 cup West Sixth Brewing Pay It Forward Cocoa Porter

In a food processor blend the garlic, onion, hot sauce, Worcestershire sauce, pepper, salt, cayenne, and mustard until smooth. Add ¼ of the grated cheddar and continue processing until smooth. Then alternate between adding the porter and the rest of cheese. When all of the beer and cheese has been added, scrape down the sides of the processor and continue to process until completely smooth.

# 3

# THE TRAIL

It's a rather warm May afternoon, and Nancy Turner and I zoom down Kentucky Highway 627 (Boonesboro Road), a busy cut-through from I-64 to I-75, on our way to Hall's on the River, an iconic stop on Winchester's Beer Cheese Trail. "The Queen of England has eaten Hall's beer cheese and had it shipped back with her," says Nancy, who is the executive director of Winchester–Clark County Tourism. "I think that was in the '80s, when she used to come in because of the horse industry." Nancy mentions that Mike McCready, lead guitarist of Pearl Jam, stopped at Hall's after playing a show in Lexington. "Those are their claims to fame," she says. We pass hilly farmlands, Blackfish Bison Ranch, and a waterfall before we end up on the verdant Kentucky River—the birthplace of beer cheese. The foundation of Allman's Fisherman's Inn is right across the street from Hall's. Despite frequent seasonal flooding, today the river is tranquil.

Many people interviewed for this book speak about Hall's on the River as a place they visited as a kid where they tried beer cheese for the first time, and a place that once provided guests with a complimentary beer cheese relish tray. The high-water mark from the flood of December 1978 delineates the hostess area. The water was so high it reached the ceiling. Hall's shows a sense of humor about the floodings, though, in its "Hall's *in* the river" display that documents news on the ravaging floods.

We're here to meet with Ms. Jean Bell, or Ma Bell, as she's affectionately known. The thing is, Ryan Curry, the manager, failed to tell her we were coming and so she's reluctant to talk to us at first—but then she loosens up. Ms. Bell started working at Hall's more than fifty years ago and used to make beer cheese every day. "Back then I made a thousand pounds a week, but someone else filled the cups," she says. Let me clarify—she made those thousand pounds *by hand*, and her hands swelled up every day. Plus, she had to do the prep for the other menu items. Incredible. She doesn't remember when Hall's "went electric" and purchased an electric mixer, which slashed her workload. Even with the new-fangled technology, she was still so busy making cheese she didn't get to meet Queen Elizabeth.

Ma Bell won't reveal the beer cheese recipe—or "pattern," as she calls it—but rattles off the ingredients: Bud Light, garlic, red pepper, and sharp cheddar cheese. "I made it to suit my taste," she says. "If I make a lot of beer cheese I get a headache—smelling the garlic, the beer, and that stuff." Luckily for her, she doesn't make the beer cheese anymore, because—gasp—Hall's outsources it to Wisconsin.

Ms. Bell fondly remembers the halcyon days, when she worked with George and Gertrude Hall and their son Steve. "They were wonderful people to work for," she says. Steve Hall ran the restaurant from 1970 to 1988, when he died from a brain tumor. In 1989 Dr. James Crase and other investors purchased the restaurant; Crase's son Karl currently owns it. At the 2015 Beer Cheese Festival, Hall's won first place in the commercial category; in 2016 they won the people's choice award. "Karl did not like the trophy he was given, so he bought a six-foot trophy and declared himself the Beer Cheese Champion of the World," Nancy says. Apparently you can just do that.

Ryan brings over a relish tray of beer cheese and also serves up the Ma Bell burger, which is smothered with beer cheese. Even though Ms. Bell has had to endure some work hardships, the restaurant honored her in naming the burger after her and giving her a parking spot with her name on it. Still, she says wistfully, "I wish I just had one cent [per pound] for all the beer cheese I've made in my life." We try to add it up in our heads—a thousand pounds a week, fifty years. "That's a lot of cheese," so the saying goes.

Instead of making beer cheese all day, Ms. Bell now preps the food and endures working with messy men. "I don't like to work with guys," she says.

She doesn't eat much of the food served at Hall's but enjoys cooking for her family, including her nephew Yeremiah Bell, who played football for the Miami Dolphins, the New York Jets, and the Arizona Cardinals. Ma Bell is a trove of Kentucky food lore. She's one of few people still alive to tell antiquated beer cheese stories, and she holds nothing back.

There isn't a starting point on the Trail, but many trail-goers begin at Winchester's Full Circle Market. The sprightly Laura Sheehan has owned the health food store for more than fifteen years. "Is beer cheese a passion of yours?" she asks me. "It's become a passion," I respond. Sheehan separates her product from the other beer cheeses by making a gluten-free one, sold in different sized grab-and-go containers. She established the beer cheese in 2010. "There's a demand in our store for gluten-free products, and I love beer cheese and it's really not the healthiest product out there," she explains. "I thought I could fill a void for people who love beer cheese and who are on gluten-free diets, because we already have a lot of people coming in here for gluten-free items." She says gluten-free food isn't just a store craze. "We've been offering gluten-free products since we opened." (They opened in 2001.) In 1995 a college friend of Sheehan's was diagnosed with celiac disease, thus gluten became "a personal interest to me." She uses a sorghum-based beer mixed with a preservative-free, no-color-added cheese, and she ages the beer cheese

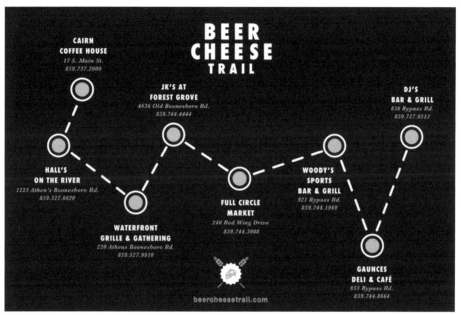

All eight destinations on Winchester's Beer Cheese Trail. (Courtesy Beer Cheese Trail)

ten days to two weeks before selling it. "I think the aging allows the flavors to blend a little better," she says. At the 2011 Beer Cheese Festival, her entry won third place in the commercial division. But in 2016 it won first prize.

Laura experimented in creating a vegan version, messing around with miso and trying a cashew base, but they aren't good enough substitutes for real cheese. In the wintertime, Sheehan makes a non-gluten-free beer cheese calls Feta-weizen: hefeweizen beer, feta, sassafras, and sweet crystallized ginger. She relays how Full Circle is "off the beer cheese radar," yet the Trail has attracted more customers to the store.

As Nancy and I exit Full Circle, we encounter a mother-daughter team touring the Trail. They gush about how they love regional foods. The Trail doesn't have much of a budget for marketing, and they discuss how great it would be to someday post one of those brown "attraction" signs along the interstate. Kentucky already attracts tourists with the Bourbon Trail, which has stops close to Winchester. Besides the Beer Cheese Trail, the state boasts several other trails, many of which have nothing to do with bourbon. The Brewgrass Trail spotlights several Central Kentucky breweries; the Western Kentucky BBQ Trail traverses from Louisville to Paducah; and the I-65 and I-75 culinary trails each comprises eateries located near or along those corridors.

To complete the Beer Cheese Trail and earn an "I Conquered the Beer Cheese Trail" T-shirt from Nancy, trail-goers must hit up at least five of the eight official spots and get stamps on their "Cheese Log," a card with all of the locations listed on it. (The logs can be found at the stops and at the Winchester tourism office.) Since Nancy activated the Trail in 2013, more than two hundred people have "conquered" it. "I think it's different," Nancy says. "One thing I like about the Trail is that on all eight stops there's not a beer cheese that tastes the same. And that's kind of unique—how one little spice or dash of this or that can make a big difference." Having your own beer cheese and making it in your own facility are the only criteria for landing on the Trail. "You can't use someone else's beer cheese," she says, which is what disqualifies Engine House Deli and Pub, because they proffer River Rat Beer Cheese, not their own.

Nancy's been with Winchester tourism for fifteen years, and she loves her job. She's good at it, too. "When we did our research last year, it was pleasantly surprising [to learn] that a lot of people intentionally come to Winchester because they have read about it." In between stops, Nancy schools me on local history, like how Winchester grows a lot of hemp. "In the '40s, we were the hemp capital of the world; we produced more hemp than anybody else," she says. Atalo Holdings, a research firm, grows hemp in Clark County on twenty-seven acres of land. With her vast store of trivia about the town she's native to, she reminds me of *Parks and Recreation*'s Leslie Knope—except without the spastic personality. Nancy seems to know everybody in Winchester, and on top of it, she's the perfect beer cheese eating companion.

In 2015 Cairn Coffee House became the latest addition to the Trail. Under the umbrella of Calvary Christian Church, the cafe opened in 2012, with a coffee shop on the first floor and a teen center on the second. The teen center evolved from a 2009 community survey that discovered that sixty to seventy students were running around town with nothing to do after school and "getting into habits that aren't ideal." Joseph Miller, Cairn's assistant manager, says, "Ultimately, the money we make down here goes to funding the teen center. That's primarily why we're open. So we're able to do a lot of good and be a reliable outreach to our community."

"Dream big" is their motto, and they proudly state that one of the students who engages in the center will be heading to culinary school soon. Their signature beer cheese sandwich, called the Hot Mess, also draws in people. Cairn's blends Natural Light beer into preshredded cheese, which is a taboo. (Most restaurants either shred a block of cheese or use cold-pack cheese; otherwise the spread gets clumpy. Also, preshredded cheese contains a high percentage of cellulose, or wood pulp, a non-nutritious filler and anticaking agent.) The Hot Mess includes bacon, Grippo's chips, beer cheese, pepperoni, and American cheese on the pressed sandwich.

"We wanted something that had local flavor," Miller says. "If you've been around Winchester at all, you know that we like two things. We like Ale-8 and

## Grilled (Beer) Cheese

Amp up mundane grilled cheese with beer cheese. You can combine the beer cheese with other cheeses if you like, or just solely use beer cheese. Heat a tablespoon of olive oil in a frying pan. Spread a layer of beer cheese on a slice of bread (locally made preferred) and add it, bread-side down, to the hot pan. Spread more beer cheese on another slice of bread for the top half. Cook, flipping frequently, until the cheese is melted and the bread is golden brown.

we like beer cheese. We were using a local beer cheese and [general manager] Luke [Toy] made the call, and I think Nancy wanted us to have our own beer cheese so we could be added to the Trail. It was good to get our own out there." During the last Beer Cheese Festival they sold about ninety Hot Messes, and they've had quite a few people visit them for the Trail. "There's obviously a demand for it," Toy says. "There are some days when that'll be the only sandwich we'll make for two straight hours. I think people really like the taste; they like having something regional and local that gives them a glimpse of what culture is around here."

"Each person who's making beer cheese adds a little flavor to it and makes it their own," Miller says. "People are taking more liberties, getting away from that original recipe." Toy has considered making a bacon beer cheese, and a jalapeño one. "I think a beer cheese latte—I don't know about that one," he jokes.

From Cairn, we drive a few miles to Woody's Sports Bar and Grill, nestled in a shopping center on Winchester's west side. It smells like bacon inside. The owner, Stacy Lisle, is "Woody." I tell him I'm writing a book about beer cheese, and he quips, "It's like Kramer [from *Seinfeld*]—a book about coffee tables." Sort of. He says he only makes batches of medium and hot beer cheeses—no mild—so he can sell more beer. Then another *Seinfeld* reference pops in my head: "These pretzels are making me thirsty." Lisle is right—his beer cheese is spicy. He sells about five to ten pounds of it a week and serves it with a basket of celery, carrots, and House Recipe Wafers. Most people have a clandestine aura when they talk about their beer cheese recipes, but Lisle flat-out grabs my notepad and jots down the recipe (see p. 57). He uses sharp cheddar cheese and Velveeta (set at room temperature), red pepper flakes, and Miller Lite.

"I actually didn't know anything about it until I moved to Winchester twenty years ago," he says. Before it was Woody's, the bar was called Peppers, and Peppers gave Stacy's friend Dave Crawley its beer cheese recipe. Crawley then passed it along to Lisle. "That's the first time I'd really ate it, and I thought, that's pretty good, so I stayed with same recipe the whole time." He jokes that the Beer Cheese Festival–winning recipe has been laminated so he can't change it.

Every beer cheese I've tried on the Trail has been completely different in taste, color, and texture. One of the best is at JK's at Forest Grove, located south of Winchester. "I changed the beer and I changed the cheese, and added a little something else," says co-owner Jennifer Phillips, who keeps improving her recipe. "I think it's ten times better than it was before. And I've made a lot of it in the past couple of weeks." She says three Trail people stopped by the day we visited and raved, "By far, yours is the best." At first she wouldn't divulge the beer she used, but I was able to break her down. Phillips switched out Corona for Country Boy Cougar Bait beer, a blonde ale. "I don't like Corona and I kept thinking, I don't drink that, I drink this. Let's try this. I like the fact that it's local beer." With the warmer weather, Phillips has seen an uptick of people doing the Trail. "I like being on the Trail," she says. "I really like people coming, just like earlier with those three people. It's rewarding to have some-body come in and want to do that, and then compliment you on it." Unlike any-one else in Winchester, Phillips serves her beer cheese on saltines with sweet pickles on top of the cheese. "That combination of the cracker, the beer cheese,

JK's at Forest Grove serves up beer cheese paired with Kentucky Ale-8. (Courtesy Hank Phillips)

and the pickle on top—it's good," Phillips says. Garlicky would be another way to describe it.

Phillips co-owns the country store/restaurant with her parents, Greg and

The Trail

Alice Keller. (JK stands for Jennifer Keller, her maiden name. "It's kind of kitschy," she says.) They put beer cheese on sandwiches like the Forest Grove Bar-B-Q, made with beer cheese, slaw, and pork on a bun. Situated in the corner of the store is a long, heavy-looking Ale-8 cooler. "Dad asked Ale-8 if they could put one in there," she says.

I ask Phillips why she thinks so many Kentuckians are obsessed with beer cheese. "It originated here so I think it's just always been a tradition. You go to another state and they're like, 'What?' 'It's cheese with beer in it. How much better could you get?' It's always been huge. I've always eaten it." Like me, she doesn't understand why beer cheese hasn't taken off outside of Kentucky. "They'd like it if they tried it. It kind of boggles me sometimes."

At this point, the late afternoon slumber sets in and we're ready for a nap. I suggest to Nancy that the Trail needs to arrange rest stops along the way so people can curl up on a bench and take a siesta. Central Kentucky has that effect on you. It just feels calmer, more relaxed than anywhere else. The open spaces, the blue skies, the patios, the businesses inside old homes—this is how life in big cities should be. With more stops to go, I don't know how I'm going to find room in my stomach for more beer cheese, and I contemplate becoming a vegan after this book is finished.

We drive five miles from JK's back into town to Gaunce's Deli, owned by John and Tiffany Gaunce. Inside the ample space they cure country ham, sell River Rat Beer Cheese, dispense Ale-8 from a soda fountain, and make a nuclear orange, annatto-dyed beer cheese. "It's a family recipe," John says. "We started making it thirty-five years ago." He uses cold-pack cheese, Bud, hot sauce, cayenne, garlic, and "some other stuff." He and Tiffany make twenty pounds at a time using an industrial mixer that's "probably as old as the beer cheese recipe." John says they sell the most beer cheese in the summertime and around the holidays. They smear some on a breakfast sandwich called the Snappy Ham and Egg Sandwich, made with their house-cured country ham, Smitty's. "We've been making country hams for sixty years," John says. "My grandfather started making those. He used to cure them, the hams. We did it in the basement of our grocery store. We cook our own hams here and sell them." The ham, with hints of clove and brown sugar, tastes rich but not too salty. Come here for the beer cheese but also pick up some ham.

Across the street from Gaunce's sits DJ's Bar and Grill. Akin to JK's, DJ's is an acronym, this time for owners Donna and Jim Crim. When we were there the couple broke the news they are partially retiring to Florida and taking beer cheese down there. They sold their six-year-old restaurant and leased a Florida restaurant half the size of DJ's. The Crims bought a house in Florida four years ago, and Donna's dad lives down there. "It fell into place, so we decided to go for it," Donna says. "Hopefully we're not messing up." She plans on making beer cheese at her new restaurant, but she ran into a snag when her high-quality Wisconsin distributor said they'll only ship it to her if she buys two thousand pounds at a time. "I have to buy a whole pallet of it," she says. "That's a lot of cheese." To make DJ's beer cheese, she uses a Hobart mixer and throws in cold-pack cheddar, beer, and spices. DJ's is known for steaks, but they sell about a hundred pounds of beer cheese a week. She showed the new owner how to make her twenty-two-year-old beer cheese recipe. "It's going to be hard to leave," she says, but Floridians will soon get a taste of Kentucky-style beer cheese—though some of the Crims' Florida neighbors are already beer cheese addicts. "My dad's neighbor is hooked on it," she says. "We got a guy who lives besides us. He's eighty-seven or eighty-eight. As soon as he sees us he gets on his lawnmower and rides over. He doesn't say 'hi' or 'how you're doing?' The first words out of his mouth are: 'Did you bring cheese?' I tell my husband, 'They're not going to be happy, because now they're going to have to pay for it.'"

With the exception of Waterfront Grille, located down the road from Hall's (the owners weren't available to see us), we finally complete the official Trail. But we have one more stop. We settle into Engine House Deli and Pub to talk with Bob Tabor, the former owner of Engine and the current owner of

Engine House's beer cheese potato chips. (Courtesy Melissa Young/Winchester–Clark County Tourism)

River Rat Beer Cheese. Clad in a Beer Cheese Festival T-shirt, the septuagenarian tells me how he became a beer cheese maker. Tabor opened the restaurant in 1984, inside Winchester's first firehouse (built in 1885), as a deli and ice cream counter. In 2015 Steve Atkins took over the Engine and revamped the menu, adding gastronome dishes like sangria fruit salad, grilled cheese with country ham, poutine made with duck-tomato-bacon gravy, potato chips smothered in beer cheese, and the River Rat Trap beer cheese platter. Atkins added a bar with several local beers on draft, hence the "pub" in the title. The bottom of the menu reads "Be cool, 'Chester.'" "I never knew we had hipsters in Winchester until I came here on a Friday night," Nancy jokes.

Tabor tells us stories while we munch on the creamy cheese, served with round pepper crackers and celery. Tabor got his start working for the Allmans in the 1970s. "I saw how they made beer cheese," he says. "Eight years later, when I opened this place up in '84, I was trying to do a nostalgia menu of items from restaurants that were no longer in business, and I would try to re-create them to the best of my memory. And strangely enough, I don't eat cheese." He grew up on a farm and cheese curds disgusted him, turning him off to most cheeses. "Only in high school, for love, did I try pizza," he continues. "This girl that I had crush on said, 'Here, try this pizza,' and I think, 'Oh man. I have to step up here.' And I like it. So I eat pizza. I don't eat cheeseburgers. Never had a grilled cheese. Cottage cheese—unh-uh. It's just one of those oddities."

Despite his personal preferences, for over thirty years Tabor has made beer cheese. He uses Bud—"that's what I drink"—and cold-pack cheddar.

## Crustless Beer Cheese Mini Quiches

Whisk 3–4 pasture-raised eggs with beer cheese and a little milk. Fold in chopped green onions, fresh herbs, diced tomatoes, and mushrooms. Grease muffin tins with butter and fill tins ⅔ full. Bake at 350°F for about 15 minutes, or until brown and puffy. Note: The quiches may puff up but deflate like a soufflé once you open the oven. Make sure not to overfill the tins.

"Cold-pack cheddar is really just cheddar cheese with some water added to it. They made it at the request of bars, because they wanted a cheese that would spread like butter at room temperature," he says. It was invented at a "club," or tavern, in Wisconsin, and the cheese was packed into crocks.[1]

Tabor prefers to weigh the spices he adds to the beer and cheese "rather than measure them by tablespoon, because you can compact a spoon or have a fluffy spoon. We found it safer and more consistent to weigh it." With the help of friends/employees H. R. and Jenny Bailey, he made eighteen thousand pounds of beer cheese in 2016, selling a third of his retail to the Liquor Barn chain.

Tabor prepared his beer cheese in-house for fifteen years before he inaugurated his retail beer cheese business in 1999. "Back then they called it Snappy Cheese, so I called it Just Like Johnnie's, and then as a subtitle I added River Rat Beer Cheese. People kept asking, 'Give me some of that River Rat Beer Cheese.' Maybe I should take a hint."

Nancy asks him if his prices differ from city to city, and he gives a good explanation. "A friend of mine had seen a study on marketing that said when people are presented with a choice of a high dollar one, a low dollar one, and a middle dollar one, they buy that middle one. And that's where I price myself. I stay above the cheap one and below the most expensive one. And it's worked pretty well. Louisville does have a price increase because of the distance."

Bob is the aforementioned river rat—a fixture on the Kentucky River. He was born two miles from Main Street. Before he got into beer cheese he worked construction, including building geodesic domes. But it all circles back to the beer cheese. Both Nancy and Steve Atkins worked for Tabor when they were in high school. "I was eighteen, maybe, and I was here by myself making cheesecake and I was drinking a beer," she reminisces. "And Bob came in and caught me. He said, 'What are you doing?' I said, 'I'm making cheesecake.' He said, 'Huh, looks like you ought to be making beer cheese.' And that's all he said, but I knew he was not happy."

"Or maybe I was mad because it wasn't two beers sitting there," he razzes.

"Or that I was underage and drinking in a restaurant," she says.

The conversation turns to Ma Bell, and Tabor says, "She's the great-grandmother of my granddaughter." As you can tell, beer cheese interlocks generations and families together. Before he owned Engine House, Atkins got his launch at Hall's, under Bell's tutelage. "I started working there when I was fifteen," he says. "She took me under her wing." She taught him how to properly make a burger. "Over time we became tight. She's tough, but such a wonderful soul."

We discuss the upcoming Beer Cheese Festival, and Bob shifts into "back in my day" cranky man. "The problem is, most of the judges, they don't have a baseline," he says. "They don't have any experience to what Allman's beer cheese tasted like. They're not old enough. As my mother-in-law used to say, 'Old as dirt to remember some of it.' So when they judge it, they're sort of judging it to their own taste, not comparing it to what the baseline should be. They had somebody in from California judging one year, and they didn't know what beer cheese was. So that makes it sort of a toss-up, really." I will be one of those judges in a couple of weeks, but I know what the "baseline" is, especially having spent hours on the Beer Cheese Trail.

The local iconoclast known as Bob Tabor excuses himself so he can "trade

Although not on the Beer Cheese Trail, Blue Isle in Winchester makes its own beer cheese. (Photo by the author)

beer cheese for moonshine," which sounds like fun. I decide I want to live in Winchester, on the Beer Cheese Trail, forever. Alas, it's time to redeem my prize—a T-shirt. At her office, Nancy hands me the shirt and I feel like an Olympian. No matter what happens to me in life I'll always have something only I and two-hundred-plus others have accomplished. It was worth every delicious minute of it.

For more on the Beer Cheese Trail, visit beercheesetrail.com.

## Seven Other Things to Do in Winchester

### 1. Try More Beer Cheese at Blue Isle Home-Style Restaurant and Bar

A half-mile from DJ's, Blue Isle isn't on the Beer Cheese Trail, but it should be. The home-style eatery serves their spicy beer cheese in an eight-ounce container surrounded by Club crackers, celery, and carrots. (They also put beer cheese on their burger.) It's a meal in itself, and if you can't finish it, you can take it with you. (facebook.com/Blue-Isle-Home-Style-Restaurant-and-Bar-1662944523988945)

### 2. Eat Local Foods at Graze Market and Café

Graze specializes in farm-to-table food and lists rotating entrees daily on a chalkboard. In offering only a few items a day, their food stays fresher. Executive Chef Craig de Villiers sources his meats from local farms, including his own. Occasionally he makes a beer cheese mac and cheese, made with local beer and cheeses and strewn with Grippo's chips. In winter 2017 Graze opened a second location, in Lexington. (facebook.com/grazelex)

## 3. Tour Blackfish Bison Ranch

Get up close and personal with American buffalo on a tour of the ranch, named after Chief Blackfish, leader of the Shawnee Indians. You can hand-feed the animals and throw a tomahawk (not at the animals). If you're squeamish about eating the animals raised on the ranch, be forewarned: you will have the option to sample buffalo meat. Reservations are required. (facebook.com/blackfishbisonranch)

## 4. Learn about Local History at Bluegrass Heritage Museum

The three-floor building spotlights Daniel Boone artifacts, a collection of quilts, and a former medical clinic. Clark County folks who served in the military are honored, and there's an exhibit on local agriculture and a collection of telephones and switchboards located in the Bell South Room. (bgheritage.com)

## 5. Get in Touch with Nature at Lower Howard's Creek Nature and Heritage Preserve

The 348-acre preserve, situated behind Hall's on the River, looks stunning in every season. Literally take a hike on the John Holder Trail and discover rare species; walk over suspension bridges and admire the natural waterfalls. Even when frozen over in winter, the creek appears magical. (lowerhowardscreek.org)

## 6. See What Kentucky Frontier Life Was Like

Only a five-mile drive from Hall's, Fort Boonesborough State Park, in Richmond, preserves Daniel Boone's 1700s history. See his reconstructed forts, buy a coonskin cap, and then take a dip in the park's junior Olympic-size pool, where Johnnie Allman once worked as a lifeguard. (parks.ky.gov/parks/recreationparks/fort-boonesborough)

## 7. Tour an Old-Fashioned Candy Factory

Twenty minutes northeast of Winchester, in Mt. Sterling, you can tour Ruth Hunt Candy, a company that's been churning out hand-pulled candies since 1921. Their specialty is the Blue Monday: a cream center encased in semisweet chocolate. (It's the official candy of the Derby.) Stop by and watch how their "real dairy" chocolates are made. (ruthhuntcandy.com)

## "A Late One"

Besides beer cheese, Winchester is famous for originating yet another addictive and fanatically revered treat: Ale-8-One ("A Late One") soda, the only soft drink invented in the Commonwealth that's still being manufactured here today. It's a drink so alluring that in 1992 the *Los Angeles Times* deemed it had "mystical properties."[2]

The magic began in 1926 when G. L. Wainscott launched his ginger- and citrus-tinged soda, after having run into legal issues with his Roxa-Kola in 1930. "He went to Holland and he went door to door and bought up ginger beer recipes, because people had—kind of like beer cheese—their very own guarded recipes, and he started making Ale-8," Nancy Turner says. "He didn't have any heirs, so the company went to his wife's nephew [Frank A. Rogers Sr.], and it's still in the family." The hand-mixed Ale-8 doesn't taste like ginger ale, but it also doesn't taste like Sprite. Akin to beer cheese (and Coke), only a handful of people know the whole recipe. In Winchester and Lexington vending machines dispense the drink, and many businesses showcase Ale-8-One signage in their windows. Ale-8 can be found all over Kentucky, but its availability is limited outside Ohio, Indiana, and East Tennessee. In 2016, however, Cracker Barrel elected to sell the beverage at forty-four of their restaurants, garnering the cult drink a larger reach. But if you don't live in the region or near a Cracker Barrel that sells it, you can order a pack of regular, diet, or caffeine-free online. (They even ship to the military.) Drinking Ale-8 out of a longneck bottle is the best way to experience the elixir, but you can also cook with it. Ale-8's website lists several recipes, from Ale-8 Can Chicken to a cocktail called the Winchester (vodka, Ale-8, and orange juice). I recommend mixing Ale-8 and bourbon together and dropping a splash into a shot of espresso, for an extra jolt. Ale-8 also manufactures their own salsas, barbecue sauces, and Sweet Heat, a nonalcoholic cheese spread made with, you guessed it, Ale-8. Those who are interested in Ale-8's production can visit the Winchester plant and watch the green bottles speed down the line à la *Laverne and Shirley* or Lucy and Ethel. (ale8one.com)

## Notes

1. Wisconsin Milk Marketing Board, eatwisconsincheese.com/cheeses/17/cold-pack.

2. Martin Booe, "A Bubbly Soft Drink's the Toast of Kentucky," *Los Angeles Times*, Dec. 14, 1992, articles.latimes.com/1992-12-14/news/mn-1535_1_soft-drink.

# 4

# THE FESTIVAL AND THE CONTEST

### Beer Cheese Festival

I first attended Winchester's Beer Cheese Festival in 2014. I stood in the lobby of city hall and presented the volunteers a beer cheese I'd made for the amateur competition. My hopes, my dreams, depended on the next few hours. However, when the winners were announced at the end of the fest, my name wasn't called. I felt crushed. In hindsight, I hadn't realized that Winchesterians prefer a certain type of beer cheese, and mine wasn't it. Flash-forward two years later; this time I return as a judge for the eighth annual festival. It's June 11, 2016, and I have the influence to crush other people's beer cheese dreams—oh, the power.

The first annual Beer Cheese Festival was "founded in response to a training [session] the Main Street Winchester [MSW] board participated in," Rachel Alexander, executive director of MSW, tells me. "The facilitator made the suggestion that we create a fundraising event that would provide us with funds for downtown projects. I'm not sure anyone knows exactly who thought of doing a Beer Cheese Festival as the fundraiser, but it was the perfect answer to the facilitator's suggestion. I don't think anyone anticipated just how successful it would be." Winchester's population is around eighteen thousand people. In 2009, the fest's inaugural year, about thirteen thousand hungry beer cheese eaters descended on downtown; in 2016 about twenty thousand came, despite 90º weather. That seems like a lot of people, but a broad swath of Kentuckians still do not know about the event. I'd been in Lexington earlier that day in June 2016, and I told a woman I was going to the Beer Cheese Festival. She said, "What's the Beer Cheese Fest?" It was her loss. Alexander says she and a staff of volunteers spend six to nine months planning the fest. "Each year we try to add something new," she says. "The festival originally consisted of just the beer cheese tasting, but it has slowly evolved to include two music stages, arts and crafts, a People's Choice Award, and a Kentucky Proud market."

The festival will mark its tenth anniversary in 2018, and the town wants it to be the "biggest and best Beer Cheese Festival ever." Alexander says, "I'm not sure what 'biggest and best' looks like, but we have an incredibly smart,

The 2016 official Beer Cheese Festival poster, designed by Ansel Petrey. (Courtesy Winchester–Clark County Tourism)

dedicated, and creative committee that will no doubt come up with something that will knock our socks off."

For some reason only nine commercial vendors showed up in 2016, as opposed to the thirteen who had signed up. In 2015 they had seventeen beer cheese makers in competition. I remember more vendors dishing out samples in 2014, as well. "One issue was definitely the heat," Alexander says. "We had a few competitors cancel at the last minute, and that was a factor."

Thankfully, as a judge in the amateur competition I get to sit inside the air-conditioned city hall while everyone sweats their faces off like Arnold Ernst Toht in *Raiders of the Lost Ark*. To my right sits a cadre of teenaged judges from Winchester, and to my left sits a transplanted Frenchman who lives in the area. The three commercial judges are situated on a dais where city officials hold business during the week. City hall is where all of the vital community business goes down, but today it's all about beer cheese. I'm not sure what the criteria are to be a beer cheese judge, but it seems like just about anyone who has tried beer cheese can do it.

For 2016 the committee decided to go electronic. I open my clunky laptop, and everyone else works on their iPads and iPhones. We have forty-four amateur samples to taste, and I only have to eat seventeen of them. The judging consists of four categories: color, consistency, smell, and taste. I ask about the color factor, and they tell me it shouldn't be either white or too orange. I think about places I'd been where beer cheese is made with white cheddar and wonder how those chefs' concoctions would fare. (They'd be demoted.) Disqualification *is* one option for judges. The beer cheese must rank at least a 5 on a scale of 0–25. If it tastes too awful to judge, you can reject it.

The judging is done as a blind tasting, so I don't know the names of the cooks or anything about their beer cheeses. Volunteers give me a few plastic cups at a time, each with a number written on it. I used to think even bad beer cheese was good—that is, until I judged the fest. I didn't ditch any of them, but a few tasted like the cook had dumped steak seasoning and/or a tablespoon of salt into the mixture. (Thank goodness for the palate-cleansing bottled water.) Is that a hint of mayo? Cranberries? Ranch seasoning? I have no idea. Some of the beers used overpowered the other flavors so much that the beer cheese tasted unpleasant.

The smell factor bewildered me a little. Most of the entries didn't have a scent—maybe that's the idea. I kept thinking about what Bob Tabor had told me: that a lot of the judges don't understand what the guideposts for beer cheese are. When I entered my beer cheese in 2014 I didn't understand, but now I do. Winchester beer cheese sets itself apart from other regional beer cheese, and that native yardstick comes with an inflexible judging system.

Basically, experimentation doesn't fly here. The commercial judges finish way before the eight amateur judges do. Because I'm meticulous, it takes me more than an hour to judge. I retry a few of them and realize they were better than I thought. Others, yeah, they still aren't worthy.

After judging, I'm free to roam around Beer Cheese Boulevard and the beer garden in the baking heat. Vendors keep their beer cheeses on ice, and despite the heat, long lines form for samples of River Rat, Hall's, and North Coast. A Kentucky Proud–sponsored stand retails all of the commercial beer cheeses in eight-ounce containers. I notice that the arts and crafts facet seems to have grown from two years ago and now usurps the beer cheese: wineries, community booths, and jewelry vendors take up most of the Main Street space. To accompany the beer cheese samples outside, Maddie's Café on Main sells beer cheese cupcakes and a pork chop smothered with Howard's Creek beer cheese.

At five p.m., on the steps of city hall, a festival official rattles off the winners. In the amateur category the top prizes go to Gary Willoughby (with Aunt Emma's Beer Cheese), Barry Profitt, and Steve Childress. (He seems to place every year.) Full Circle Market, River Rat, and Moo Shine win in the commercial contest, and the outsourced Hall's takes people's choice. I have no clue if any of the amateur beer cheeses I ranked high won, and I'll never know

Beer Cheese Blvd. in Winchester—heart of the annual Beer Cheese Festival. (Courtesy Adam Kosobud)

Thousands of people converge on downtown Winchester for the eighth annual Beer Cheese Festival in 2016. (Courtesy Adam Kosobud)

whose was whose. Some people who win the festival go on to sell their product commercially, as was the case with 2010 amateur winner, Olivia's Beer Cheese (see chapter 6). Winning a trophy and money gives these beer cheese "chefs" confidence to take the next step. Who will be the next beer cheese star? (beer-cheesefestival.com)

## Country Boy Brewing Beer Cheese Contest

Although Winchester's Beer Cheese Festival boasts rigorous judging guidelines, the annual beer cheese contest conducted by Lexington's Country Boy Brewing allows home cooks and professional chefs the leeway to almost throw in the kitchen sink. I don't know why Winchester has more rigid guidelines, but I can speculate it's because they take their heritage very seriously. And when you hold a contest at a brewery, the culture is automatically going to be lax. Held in mid-May, during Lexington Craft Beer Week, Country Boy's contest acts as a warm-up to Winchester's big festival. Unlike the Beer Cheese Festival, Country Boy doesn't assign judges—contest-goers vote for their two favorites. In one way, it's more democratic, but you do get to meet the beer cheese makers and talk with them about their creations, which could factor into your picks.

Country Boy taproom manager Zac Wright helped organize the first annual contest in 2013. "One day we convinced Dad's Favorites [based in Lexington] to make a batch with one of our beers [Stampin' Ground, a nitro stout] and it ended up being one of their top sellers," Wright says. "From there, we thought about who else could use our beer to make beer cheese. We thought we'd hold a small competition. The first year we got fifteen entrants. The second year we got forty-two, and this year [2016] we're looking at somewhere around sixty." It's mandatory for contestants to use a Kentucky-brewed beer, so most select a Country Boy beer like the habanero-infused Nacho Bait. Halfway Home Pale Ale, Jalapeño Smoked Porter, and Shotgun Wedding (a brown ale) are also popular choices. "There's nothing more Kentucky than beer cheese," Wright says.

Most of the entrants are amateurs—none of the entrants seem to live outside of Kentucky—but professional chefs participated in about ten of the groups, including people who work at Connemara Golf Course, Red State BBQ, County Club restaurant, Apollo Pizza, and the Gastro Gnomes food truck. Wright says in 2015 more than six hundred people came to sample homemade beer cheeses; that number more than doubled in 2016 to fifteen hundred tasters. "It's getting to be quite a hassle," he says. "I've answered upwards of three hundred emails for this event. It's a lot of verbatim." The event has traditionally been held in their warehouse across the street from their taproom, but in February 2017 the brewery opened a five-million-dollar expansion in Georgetown that includes a twenty-thousand-square-foot building to accommodate more room for production and a taproom. Management has considered moving the event outdoors for future beer cheese contests, and they've discussed capping the entrants at fifty beer cheese teams.

In 2016 the entrance fee is only five dollars, and all of the money goes to a local charity. This year it's for Old Friends, a farm where retired thorough-breds live (see chapter 5). Unlike the Beer Cheese Festival, the beer cheeses here aren't for sale. I enter Country Boy's facility and feel overwhelmed by the number of people gathered at the tables that snake through the space. I'd compare the vibe to the magnitude of any sort of fanboy/fangirl convention. It's then I realize how cult-like beer cheese is. The team names are clever and funny, such as Beer Cheesus Christ, Here for the Beers, Blair's F*cking Awe-some Cheez, and my personal favorite, New Cheese on the Block. Contest-goers are given a piece of paper to write down their favorites as they graze each sta-tion and scoop up the cheeses using celery, carrots, crackers, and pretzels as delivery systems.

"I think everybody has a family recipe for beer cheese," Wright says. "People are interested in getting it out. There are so many different styles. A cold, smoked white cheddar beer cheese won in 2015, which is untraditional. For most beer cheeses, you're looking at orange cheddar."

I make the rounds and talk to every single team, and everyone has a story. Some made beer cheese for the first time ever the night before the event. Some have dogged devotion to their family recipes and have been perfecting them for double decades. Some are using the contest as a harbinger to see if they should retail their product or enter it into the Beer Cheese Festival.

(Unfortunately, the people with such high expectations do not place.) Blue Horse Beer Cheese serves theirs with bread-and-butter pickles on top. Others are here as an excuse to drink and take Monday off. I get the impression many of the candidates haven't left the taproom all weekend.

Many of the entrants like their beer cheese very spicy and use backyard-grown chili peppers. Keith Moll of Hot Ticket Beer Cheese tells me he added *togarashi*, a spicy Japanese seasoning, to his beer cheese, along with pink sea salt from Afghanistan. "I try to make it simple," he says. "Last year I made it too hard. So the simpler I got, I think the better it got." Moll isn't alone in his love for heat. Chipotle peppers, *pasilla negro* chili peppers, ancho chilies, jalapeños soaked for four days in beer, and ghost peppers rear their ugly heads in the beer cheeses. Ty Bobb and his buddies (team Beer Cheesus Christ) added dill to theirs, and he tells me they decided to enter the contest because one night "we were really drunk." Several people I talk to have entered this contest before, but others are first-timers.

The Traylor sisters of Sisters' Southern beer cheese make theirs with Country Boy Cougar Bait, red pepper, garlic, sharp cheddar, and onion. This is their first year at the event, and they want to take it to the Beer Cheese Festival. "We used to make it and take it to parties," Madeline Traylor says. "We're hoping to sell it, and this is a good place to start."

## Beer Cheese Wraps

Spread a layer of beer cheese on a tortilla. Top with sliced veggies and lunch meats and roll it together.

I talk to Todd and Alan Waits. The latter is an older gentleman who doesn't appreciate the rise of gourmet beer cheese. "It's kind of getting away from what it was originally designed for," he says. Todd guns to retail his beer cheese, too, but that plan depends on whether it wins today or not. Adjacent to the Waits sits Sandra Williams, under the name Corner Tavern. She and her kinfolk have spent two decades perfecting the family beer cheese recipe. Williams decided to enter the contest based on friendly advice: "People for years have been telling me you need to start getting into some of these contests." Hers is made with some heat, but not too much. "I like it warm to the taste [as in spiciness], but not so warm it's overwhelming," she says. "It should linger for a few minutes but go away. I want it to lay on the tongue and not burn you up." She ruminates entering the Beer Cheese Festival, but like the Waits, her position at the end of this contest factors into it. We discuss how beer cheese needs to evolve outside of Central Kentucky. "Beer cheese is kind of a hidden treasure," she says. "I would like to see the rest of the country get on board."

More than half of the entrants' beer cheeses seem to contain Country Boy beers, but some use Kentucky Ale and others use beers brewed by Rooster Brewing, from Paris, Kentucky (see p. 115). Some stick to traditional beer cheese, but many others take a gourmand path, leading people to invent unthinkable combinations. Chefs Andrew Suthers and Kyle Klatka of Lexington-based Gastro Gnomes don't currently have beer cheese on their menu, but they decided to create a recipe for the contest. Klatka tells me he put Quiche My Ass beer (a Belgian pale ale from Rooster Brewing), feta, goat cheese, sundried tomatoes, basil, and pesto into a Ninja blender and blended it. He had the day off and decided to go for it. "I got it done in an hour," he says.

Kathleen Fox of Amato's Beer Cheese (she won second place) began making her beer cheese in 2011. "We grew up eating Hall's beer cheese," she says. "My sister's best friend was Steve Hall. When they sold the restaurant [the new management] changed the beer cheese and it just wasn't the same. So I thought, I'm just gonna start making it myself." In a curious move, she added three types of beers: Country Boy, Kentucky Ale, and Stella Artois. The beers give the cheese a certain sweetness, and the spices evoke a delayed zip. A second food-truck entrant, Buddy's World Famous, from Nicholasville, uses two Country Boy beers, Mexican-blend cheeses, pepper jack, Colby cheese, and ancho chilies. Buddy Hasty winged the recipe and made two separate batches and mixed them together.

# The Festival and the Contest

Things get weirder from here. Stephen Wilson combines Whole Foods–brand cheese, Country Boy Nacho Bait beer, toasted cumin, white pepper, coriander, smoked paprika, mustard seeds, and chili peppers for his submission. The seasonings give it a hummus flavor. "I went two hours, at different variables, with the KitchenAid mixer and the Vitamix blender and damn near burned up two motors to make it," he says. Using lavender, Taleggio cheese, honey, and cardamom, Steven Riddle made the oddest entry of the fest. It's distinctive, for sure, but it doesn't taste like beer cheese. He says, "It's very different," and laments that he put too much cardamom in it.

You do have to hand it to people for their limitless creativity and anything-goes approaches. Moving down the line, almost to the end, I come across Blair's F*cking Awesome Cheez from Blair Crabtree. "I've never found any other states that appreciate beer cheese as much as Kentucky," she says. "We are beer cheese connoisseurs around here." She entered the contest because every Sunday she makes beer cheese for her husband and thought it'd be a fun to participate. "I bake homemade pretzels and make beer cheese, and that's what we have for dinner on Sundays. And then beer cheese for the rest of the week."

Red State BBQ is here. They tell me they entered the contest "because we think we have damn good beer cheese and we love Country Boy." They are accurate—their beer cheese is spicy, creamy, and pairs well with their barbecue sauces. (It's worth noting that a barbecue food trailer in Nashville called the Gambling Stick also makes a Kentucky-style beer cheese to match their meats.)

I then reach Lori and Jeff McKinnery, who tell me today was only the second time they had ever made beer cheese. It was for a good cause, and they wanted to try something new, they say. In November 2015 their Southwest Chicken chili won first place at Country Boy's chili contest, and they thought they could perform well in this food group, too. New Cheese on the Block couple Brian and Lauren Hortin wanted to enter last year, but Lauren's schoolwork kept them away. Their entry features jalapeños they pickled themselves, which formed a slow burn on the tongue. They're moving to Indianapolis at the end of the week and want to seize the opportunity. "This is the first time and probably last," Lauren says. "Why the hell not?"

All of the contestants made a cold, Kentucky-style beer cheese—except for Jeff and Jennifer Mize of Just Keep Livin'. They offer a dip warmed in a slow cooker. "We're German and that's the only way you have beer cheese," Jeff says. "We're a little different, we know." They tell me they're confident Germany invented warm beer cheese, but I haven't found any evidence to support the claim.

## The Festival and the Contest

After all of that consumption, the crowd hands in their ballots. Jay Baughman and Evan and Courtney Sizemore (of Blue Horse Beer Cheese) and Kathleen Fox (of Amato's) are announced first- and second-place winners, respectively. The first-place winners receive a custom stained-glass ribbon with Country Boy's logo painted inside (a two-hundred-dollar value), and Fox wins a private tour for four to Buffalo Trace Distillery in Frankfort. To those who didn't win: keep experimenting—and remember, there's always next year. (Country Boy Brewing, shopcountryboybrewing.com)

# 5

# RESTAURANTS AND BARS

Central Kentucky is teeming with restaurants that serve homemade beer cheese. Venture outside of the middle of the state and beer cheese becomes scarce (and when it is seen, the product is typically nothing like Kentucky-style). I spent a lot of time researching (i.e., eating) different beer cheeses—both hot and cold— throughout Kentucky, Ohio, Illinois, and New York City, and I noticed Winchester beer cheese differs from Louisville beer cheese, and NYC differs from both of them. It's worth noting Winchester's beer cheese frequently comes with hard pretzels, not soft pretzels. However, Lexington and Louisville subscribe to the German-style soft pretzels, and many establishments serve both soft pretzels and crudités. But in tasting these regional beer cheeses, I found practically every one used different cheeses, beers, and spices. Of course, I'm not aware of all beer cheeses in these regions, and as far as warm beer cheese goes, I've only included places that I thought trumped other prosaic warm dips. In this chapter I give shout-outs to restaurants that I think make beer cheeses worth traveling for and that formulate singular techniques, especially regarding what they serve alongside the beer cheese (bacon-fat pretzels, anyone?).

# Lexington

The Horse Capital of World is awash with beer, beer cheese, and bourbon—sometimes fused together. A mere thirty minutes west of Winchester, Lexington continues its beer cheese traditions in breweries and restaurants. Ethereal Brewing and West Sixth Brewing depend on local beer cheese artisans to fashion exclusive beer cheese for their taprooms. Kentucky Beer Cheese uses Ethereal's Lambda Oatmeal Stout for a special blend, and Olivia's Beer Cheese takes West Sixth's IPA and produces beer cheese for both West Sixth taprooms—including downtown's Greenroom branch—where the cheese is paired with Sunrise Bakery's baguette chips.

West Sixth's flagship brewery conjoins Smithtown Seafood, owned by Ouita Michel. (She also owns Midway's Holly Hill Inn, Windy Corner Market, Wallace Station, and the Midway Bakery). Jon Sanning is the executive chef at Smithtown; he uses West Sixth's Pay It Forward Cocoa Porter to create his beer cheese. Most beer cheeses are crafted with lighter beers, so using the porter gives the beer cheese a viscous texture and a whiter shade. In approaching his beer cheese, Sanning wanted to apply a beer from West Sixth, but when Smithtown first opened the brewery had limited options.

"I definitely didn't want to do it with an IPA or the Lemongrass Wheat," Chef Sanning says, so he settled on the porter. "In the beginning, you get that dark, rich flavor, and on the backside you get the normal beer cheese, garlic, and onion flavors." He serves the beer cheese with seasonal vegetables and croustades (puff pastry). Although they specialize in catfish, tilapia, and po-boys, Smithtown also features burgers on the menu, which is why Sanning begat the beer cheese. "We were looking over the options for . . . toppings as far as burgers go," Sanning says. "It's like, oh yeah, beer cheese, of course. It was a no-brainer."

## Beer Cheese Quesadillas

Spread beer cheese on a tortilla and place the tortilla, cheese side up, in an preheated, lightly oiled skillet. Cover the cheese with another tortilla. Cook over medium heat, flipping until the tortillas are crisp and brown and the cheese is melted. Feel free to add crumbled meat, onions, and peppers to the quesadilla. Better yet, make your own flour tortillas.

Before joining Smithtown, he spent a year working at locally focused market/restaurant Windy Corner Market, located fifteen minutes north of Smithtown. He says Windy's beer cheese is made with Velveeta, bourbon, and Alltech Lexington Brewing Company's Kentucky Bourbon Barrel Ale. The piquant dip is served warm, with pretzels, and has a rather ribboned consistency. Using "cheese food" makes the beer cheese pliable, which is why a lot of purveyors use it in their beer cheeses. "There are a lot of great ones out there, even though they utilize the processed cheese," he says. "I kind of like ours now."

At Smithtown, Sanning eschews processed cheese and instead selects a New York State sharp white cheddar. "Making [beer cheese] from scratch was a big trial and error, but eventually we got the ratio worked out," he says. "We still fidget with it occasionally." They sell about fifteen pounds a week. "For the size of the restaurant that we are, it's a pretty good track record."

Unlike some other chefs, Sanning had no problem handing me his beer cheese recipe (see p. 59). "I don't understand the whole oh-no-my-recipe's-a-secret thing," he says. "I can guarantee you that they're almost all basically the same. When you're talking about emulsifying beer into cheese, or any sort of emulsification, everybody's ratios are going to be about the same."

Sanning lived in Oregon on and off, and he's puzzled as to why the area doesn't have beer cheese. "It makes no sense why nobody's making beer cheese out there, because it's such a great product," he says. "Maybe I'll just pack up and move out there and make a bunch of beer cheese. People . . . buy Cheez Whiz and garbage like that. It's like, 'No, you need to try beer cheese.'"

A cluster of no-frill places in downtown Lexington within walking distance of each other makes it easy to put together your own mini beer cheese trail. Limestone Blue sells a smoky beer cheese punctuated with Country Boy Shotgun Wedding beer, smoked paprika, and chipotle peppers that fire a spicy finish. They serve the velvety beer cheese on a tray arranged with celery and carrots and house-made soft spinach tortilla "chips" sliced into isosceles triangles. They also put the stuff on their shoestring fries, on a chicken sandwich called Southwell's Beer Cheese, and on Saturdays they offer beer cheese mac and cheese.

Saul Good—not to be confused with Saul Goodman of *Better Call Saul* and *Breaking Bad*—is only a five-minute walk from Limestone Blue. You're here for the steak and beer cheese nachos. Jalapeños, cilantro, scallions, grilled steak, beer cheese, and five melted cheeses are piled atop blue tortilla chips. The giant-portion nachos look sloppy, but they're tasty enough.

Next, sidle up to Parlay Social for their eclectic bourbon selection, Bootleg beer cheese, and Bootleg beer cheese nachos, piled with Italian sausage.

## Beer Cheese Burgers

Beer cheese makes a fantastic condiment. Instead of melting American cheese on top of a burger patty, smear a tablespoon or so of beer cheese on a toasted bun and place the bun on the meat patty as soon as you remove it from grill or skillet. For extra cheesiness, add beer cheese to both the top and bottom of the bun.

The creamy, four-ounce serving of Bootleg comes with baby carrots, Captain's Wafers, and celery and has an inkling of smokiness. Parlay doesn't make their Bootleg beer cheese in-house but instead sources it from Kentucky Beer Cheese.

Across town in the Idle Hour Shopping Center, sports bar O'Neill's (not an Irish bar) offers beer cheese that has a nacho cheese–like consistency and a neon-orange color. The tray is laced with Ritz crackers, green olives, cucumber slices, and tortilla chips. A few of the sandwiches listed on their sports-themed AFC and NFL menu come with beer cheese slathered between the buns.

Similar to Smithtown Seafood, Chatham's Southern Comfort Food puts Pay It Forward Cocoa Porter in their beer cheese, but because of the surfeit of cream cheese, it doesn't have the same dark hue. Order the charcuterie platter—country ham, andouille sausage, pimento cheese, and beer cheese. I liked the pimento cheese better than the beer cheese, which wasn't spicy enough for my taste. The crostinis don't break in the thick-as-molasses spread, but the crackers do. However, I commend Chatham's for their novel idea of marrying two Southern favorites together.

A five-minute walk from Chatham's, the Julep Cup—located beneath the Woodlands condoplex—is another restaurant specializing in Southern vittles. Chef Lindsay Brooks Brugh's beer cheese is made with Country Boy Cougar Bait, Wisconsin's Schreiber cold-pack sharp cheddar, onion powder, garlic powder, cayenne, Worcestershire sauce, Tabasco, salt, and pepper, and it has a silky texture. The stately dining room lionizes horse racing and Churchill Downs with a plethora of framed horse photos hanging on the scarlet walls, and their Seahorse Lounge plays off the horse and nautical theme with horses and seahorses tchotchkes, sometimes combined. Living up to the restaurant's namesake, their logo features a merry fox drinking a Mint Julep. Horses, seahorses, and foxes—only in the Horse Capital.

Finally, either on your drive in or out of Lexington, hit up Red State BBQ, on the outskirts of town. Its glowing lights beckon you inside the small restaurant to try the beer cheese, which they tell me "sells like crazy." They smother their grits with beer cheese, serve it on their double-stuffed brisket, and offer it as a side with four mini-sized pretzels, adding a Kentucky twist to barbecue.

## Five Other Things to Do in Lexington

With the glut of bourbon, beer, and horses, finding yourself in Lexington means you won't be bored. In April and October, Keeneland Racecourse attracts horse lovers, and anytime of the year the Kentucky Horse Park merits a visit. But if you've eaten all the beer cheese you can handle and now crave something more nourishing—like maybe a cup of coffee and free art—here are a few alternative activities.

### 1. Drink Craft Coffee

Get a jolt of caffeine (and philanthropy) at A Cup of Common Wealth, near the central business district. Try the Brewshine—cold-brew coffee steeped in bourbon-barrel char—or pore over their list of coffees procured from national roasters. If you're feeling grateful, use their Pay It Forward Board to purchase a stranger a drink. Take your beverage across the street to Thoroughbred Park and view Gwen Readon's stunning bronze racehorse sculptures. (acupof commonwealth.com)

Visit one of the North Lime Coffee & Donuts locations and pair a delicious made-from-scratch doughnut (like the funnel cake doughnut) with a Shakey Nate: locally roasted coffee, cream, and espresso shaken up. (northlime.net)

If you haven't found your java fix yet, mosey over to Daily Offerings Coffee Roastery, a commodious downtown coffeehouse specializing in its own roasts, beer, and live music. (dailyofferingscoffee.com)

For late-night coffee and food, Common Grounds is open until midnight every night. (commongroundsoflexington.com)

## 2. Eat Beer Cheese in the Woods

Kentucky Native Café is a hidden enclave situated behind Michler's Florist. To get to the café you must traipse through the greenhouse until you end up in a wooded area filled with picnic tables. The café sells German-style beers and *obatzda*, which is a traditional German cheese spread similar to beer cheese. Typically, *obatzda* doesn't contain any beer, but because we're in Kentucky the café adds a splash of it to the soft cheeses, giving the spread a yellowish hue. The café closes during the winter, but spring through fall it's a convivial destination to revel in food, drinks, and nature. (michlers.com/pages/café)

## 3. Get Loopy at the Kentucky for Kentucky Fun Mall

Some Kentuckians know the story of Pablo EskoBear, a.k.a. the Cocaine Bear, but those from outside the region might not have heard about the strange tale—

until now. Former Lexington narcotics officer Drew Thornton had $15 million in cocaine strapped to him when he jumped from a plane and his parachute didn't open. A bear came upon the drugs and consumed them, thinking it was food. The bear, of course, died of an overdose. After the taxidermied bear traveled around the U.S. for a while, the Kentucky for Kentucky organization finally secured the drugged-out ursine. Kentucky for Kentucky sells kitschy Kentucky apparel and goods—a beer cheese–scented candle, a KFC-scented candle, shirts that say "Y'all" on them, a "George Clooney Is a Beautiful Man" T-shirt, and horse socks—at their North Lexington shop, next to poor Pablo. Come and get your picture taken with a part of Kentucky's eldritch history. (kyforky.com)

## 4. Stay at the 21c Museum Hotel

Louisville and Cincinnati already have theirs, but in April 2016 downtown Lexington got a 21c Museum Hotel, too. Throughout several floors, the museum section exhibits rotating art collections in their galleries, which are free to the public. The first-floor restaurant, Lockbox, cooks up Kentucky carp (eat more carp) and other Southern-tinged dishes. If you check in for the night, your room's minibar will be stocked full of bourbon, local beer, and Ale-8, and unlike most minibars, this one is affordable. Oh, and speaking of Kentucky's favorite son, George Clooney, each room comes equipped with a Nespresso machine.

(Clooney is their spokesman.) If you do want a beer cheese snack, West Sixth Greenroom is a couple of doors down, where you can indulge in Olivia's Beer Cheese and a pint of craft beer. (21cmuseumhotels.com/Lexington)

### *5. Become a Beer, Bourbon, and Ice Cream Scholar*

Tucked away in an industrial park, the Pepper Campus once distilled James E. Pepper whiskey. Today it's a thriving food hall full of grub and booze behind a Crank and Boom Ice Cream Lounge storefront. They also have Middle Fork Kitchen Bar's "from the fire"-cooked food, Ethereal Brewing, Barrel House Distilling, Goodfellas Pizzeria, and the Break Room, a bar that overlooks the Town Branch Creek. Bring your dog to sit outside at Ethereal while you drink a beer and eat beer cheese. The campus aspect makes it seem like a school—a school of good, local stuff. (peppercampus.com)

## Five Excursions Near Lexington

### *1. Drink a Pint at Rooster Brewing*

Believe it or not, Paris, Kentucky, is, well, the Paris of Central Kentucky. Take the idyllic Kentucky Highway 627 from Winchester to Paris and end up in downtown

Paris twenty-five minutes later. Or start in Lexington and drive thirty minutes northeast on US Highway 68. Rooster was the first brewery to open in Bourbon County. Owned by local businessman Ralph Quillin, the microbrewery sells beer cheese, along with their own brews like Sleepy Puppy Belgian Pale Ale and Pretty Nice Blonde Golden Ale. Stickers from every brewery imaginable glom to the walls, generating a well-worn aesthetic. (roosterbrew.com)

## 2. Visit the Retired Horses at Old Friends Thoroughbred Farm

North of Lexington, Georgetown's blue-green pastures and ponds offer a good home for the retired thoroughbreds that live at this nonprofit farm. When their racing careers are over, the horses are literally put out to pasture. At Old Friends, Michael Blowen cares for more than 160 horses and even accepts champion stallions, thus keeping the horses away from the slaughterhouse. Horses aren't the only animals that live here. Several cats greet you as you enter the gift shop, including Bobby's Kitten, named after the 2014 Breeders' Cup–winning horse. Reservations are required for a tour of the facility. (oldfriendsequine.org)

## 3. Drink Vino at Equus Run Vineyards

If you're going to own a winery in Kentucky, it might as well be horse-themed. Cynthia Bohn instituted the winery in 1998, helping to launch Kentucky's thriving wine industry. Located in Midway, a few miles from Old Friends, Equus is exactly what a winery in Kentucky should be: gazebos, a giant Adirondack chair, vineyards in the distance, a tiered deck, live music in the summer, and a tasting room pouring sweet and dry varietals like Equestrian Chardonnay, White Riesling, and Passionate Kiss. And, of course, they sell beer cheese. (equusrunvineyards.com)

## 4. Dine at the Holly Hill Inn

Also in Midway, Chef Ouita Michel uses whatever is in season at Holly Hill, a high-end restaurant located in a restored 1845 farmhouse. It sits on a secluded lot in a residential area and offers brunch and dinner. Antiques and artwork complement the dining room, and out back they grow some of their herbs and food in a garden. Their back-to-basics approach includes a rotating menu of local meats, themed dinners, and a Southern, three-course brunch prix fixe. (hollyhillinn.com)

## 5. Explore the Jim Beam Nature Preserve

Visiting Central Kentucky means you're never too far from a distillery—or a nature preserve. Although the name evokes bourbon flowing like waterfalls, the nature preserve is only related to bourbon by its namesake. In 1995 the Jim

Beam Company (in conjunction with the Nature Conservancy) developed the 115-acre preserve, which is located in the Palisades region, near the Kentucky River in Jessamine and Garrard Counties. The preserve houses rare salamanders and snails, federally listed endangered bats, a violet-shaded flower called the starry cleft phlox, and chinquapin oak trees situated on breathtaking bluffs. (Nicholasville; nature.org/ourinitiatives/regions/northamerica/unitedstates/kentucky/placesweprotect/jim-beam-nature-preserve.xml)

## Harrodsburg and Danville

Beaumont Inn in Harrodsburg, about forty-five minutes southwest of Lexington, is Kentucky's oldest family-operated bed-and-breakfast country inn. The Dedman family runs an elegant dining room at the inn and also operates two smaller, casual pubs (where you'll find beer cheese): Old Owl Tavern and its upstairs bourbon bar, Owl's Nest Lounge, which is rated as one of the best bourbon bars in the Bluegrass. The lounge accommodates ages eighteen and up and is quieter than the downstairs restaurant. Of all the beer cheeses I tried in restaurants, the Old Owl's version probably had the boldest flavors.

Co-owner Dixon Dedman tells me Beaumont's chef, Jerry Broderick, is a "big beer cheese junkie." Broderick concurs. "A girlfriend and I, many, many moons ago, she wanted to make beer cheese, and it's something we whipped up together," he says. "It's been twisted and tweaked. Over the years, as taste buds changed, it got a little spicier; it got a little more beer in it. The beer in it has changed a few times. Before, we used anything from AmberBock to Guinness and Bass." Currently, they're using Kentucky Ale. Chef Broderick combines garlic, cayenne, paprika, and Tabasco with a cold-pack cheddar. The beer cheese comes out creamy because of the high amount of beer. He says he makes a gallon and a half every eight days. I ask him why beer cheese recipes are so clandestine: "Most chefs are secret about most their stuff," he says. "We worked hard to make it, and it's kind of our thing. There are some things we're secret about, and some things we're not, really. [The beer cheese], that's a signature kind of thing." (He did not share his recipe.)

Baked pretzels accompany the beer cheese at the Old Owl, but not the classic kind of pretzels—these are pretzels baked in bacon fat. "We were looking at the traditional choices—doing celery, carrots, crackers—and we found these Bavarian pretzel rolls. But they weren't salty enough, so we salted them and they still weren't what we wanted," says Dedman. "What's better than a little bacon grease or bacon fat?" Broderick reserves the bacon grease leftover from sizzling Hot Browns and brushes the pretzels rolls with the fat. "We have so much bacon fat leftover, and one day [we were] just sitting around," Brod-

## Beer Cheese Pizza

Make your pizza dough as usual, but substitute beer cheese for the tomato sauce. You may need to dilute the beer cheese with a little milk to spread it. Add toppings of your choice, such as bacon, caramelized onions or leeks, pepperoni, mozzarella, and fries.

erick says. "I was like—it was one of those slow days—I wonder if we could put bacon fat on those pretzels and bake them off. We did that, and we looked at each other: there it is. That's how all awesome things are created—out of boredom."

After the bacon fat cooks into the rolls, the kitchen slices them thin and serves them on a clear platter, next to a bowl of creamy beer cheese. Surprisingly, the bacon fat doesn't overpower the pretzels. Because of the Owl's Nest's immense bourbon selection—including the family's revived Kentucky Owl—I suggest ordering a Manhattan, too.

While you're in Harrodsburg you might as well visit Danville, which is ten miles south. In the spirit of Harrodsburg, Danville burbles with bourbon, beer, and beer cheese. Beer Engine sells theirs in a plastic four-ounce pack. They tell me they prefer to use dark beers, like their Virtue Porter or a milk stout. It's somewhat spicy, and you can see flecks of shredded cheese that did not mix in with the cream cheese. Afterward, take a stroll around the neighborhood to Jane Barleycorn's, yet another prized Kentucky bourbon bar. They pay homage to Kentucky's heritage by hanging up paintings of Colonel Sanders, Hunter S. Thompson, and Muhammad Ali. Stop by Burke's Bakery, Elmwood Inn Fine Teas, the Great American Dollhouse Museum, Wilderness Trail Distillery, and view a medical center named after Ephraim McDowell, who in 1809 became the first person to successfully remove an ovarian tumor.

## Louisville

Located an hour and a half northwest of Danville, Derby City's motto is "Keep Louisville Weird," but it should be "Keep it weird . . . with beer cheese." The city's languid, good-natured ambiance is comparable to another beery Southern town: Austin, Texas. In exploring Louisville's beer cheese scene, I noticed a lot of the beer cheese seems to be salmon-colored. Against the Grain, Holy Grale, Gralehaus, and Monnik Brewing Company have lighter-hued beer cheeses because they use white cheddar dyed pinkish by hot sauce. The ubiquity of salmon-hued beer cheese separates Louisville from Winchester and its yellow-orange beer cheese. Like I said, Louisville is strange.

Gralehaus chef Andy Myers is one of the locals who subscribes to the pinkish beer cheese (see recipe, p. 39). "Everybody's beer cheese is different," he says. "I think that Louisville's definitely got a beer cheese scene, for sure. I feel like it's everywhere." He serves his glossy spread in a ramekin and tops it with chives. It's so burnished it looks like it could be gelato. "I've been making some variation of that beer cheese for a long time because I like cold beer cheese better than warm beer cheese," Myers says. "When I started working for this company, I really liked Josh [Lehman's] beer cheese over at Holy Grale, and mine was pretty similar. That was kind of cool—both of us were coming from the same direction at the time." However, Holy Grale's beer cheese is chunkier than Gralehaus's. Lori Beck and Tyler Trotter own both Gralehaus and Holy Grale, and the two restaurants are linked by a shared patio. Gralehaus opened in 2014 as a daytime lunch and coffee spot, replete with beer cheese and pimento cheese on the menu. Myers uses either local Kenny's Farmhouse white cheddar or New York aged white cheddar and a bitter beer. "I like to use something hoppy in my beer cheese, because I like the bitter and the hot together," he says.

To get the beer cheese to shine, Myers lets the mixture spend at least ten minutes spinning in a food processor. He cribbed the long mixing time from Lehman, though Lehman doesn't use a food processor. "I love how creamy it is," Myers says. "You don't really have any texture of shredded cheese in it. It's just this smooth, homogenous thing." Before he started at Gralehaus, he learned the ropes in Holy Grale's kitchen. Holy Grale's and Gralehaus's beer cheeses are served with pretzels made by Klaus Riedelsheimer. "He's been in this town forever," says Meghan Levins, chef at Monnik Beer Company. Monnik uses Klaus's pretzel rolls for their sandwiches. "Everyone knows Klaus," Levins says. "He's super German. That's all he does is make pretzel bread. That really makes Holy Grale's beer cheese stand out, too. It's a decision to serve a high-quality bread like that with the beer cheese. I think that makes it ultra special." Riedelsheimer proofs the dough for at least twelve hours and imports the lye he uses from Germany.

Myers prefers cold beer cheese to warm, namely because of the effect warming has on the ingredients. "No matter what kind of beer you put in a warm beer cheese, you really just don't taste the beer," he says. "It tastes like a slightly bitter queso dip. It doesn't taste like beer cheese to me. Cold beer cheese—you can taste everything that's in it. The heat doesn't mask anything. The cheese comes across so much more, and it tastes like what it is."

"When I worked at Taco Punk, people would get mad because they thought they were getting Kentucky beer cheese because we called it queso cerveza," Levins says. "But it's queso. It's not really beer cheese."

It's safe to say a lot of Kentuckians prefer their beer cheeses cold, with the exception of one of Levins' friends. "My friend, she's the general manager of Garage Bar," Levins says. "She loves beer cheese, and so anywhere we go she gets it, and to see her little hissy fit when it comes out cold. I tell her, 'It's just cheese. Eat it!'"

Eiderdown, in Germantown, makes a tangy, warm beer cheese. Chef Brian Morgan uses white cheddar and seasonal beer, and his isn't too spicy. Monnik—which is the sister brewery to Danville's Beer Engine—is another Germanic brewpub. It opened in 2015 in the Schnitzelburg neighborhood. Levins shores up her beer cheese with house-made spent-grain bread (using the leftover malt from brewing). She salvages the grains, makes a focaccia-like dough, and folds in the ingredients by hand. "I didn't want to do a pretzel bread, because that's what everyone else is doing it," she says.

She says her recipe is based on the one from Beer Engine, which was created by one of the owners' wives. "I didn't even want to put beer cheese on the menu, believe it or not, because it was cliché," Levins says. "And one of the owners said, 'You just need to try the beer cheese. Trust me, it's different enough.'" Levins agreed, and now she makes ten pounds a day. The recipe contains cream cheese, cayenne, a Wisconsin sharp cheddar cheese, onion, and a light Monnik beer, all blended in a food processor. Besides serving it as an appetizer, she also puts the beer cheese on their burger.

Louisville isn't just cool, pink, Kentucky-style beer cheese. The menu for Bluegrass Brewing Company (BBC) lists "beer cheese," but it's a warm dip delivered with a pretzel. (They do sell a carryout cold version at their location, but it's not listed on the menu.) Crescent Hill Craft House also sell "beer cheese." Again, theirs is a tepid, milky dip served with a house-made pretzel. The lesson is: ask if the beer cheese comes warm or cold, because you will be mad if you want cold and get warm, and vice versa.

In further digging through Louisville's beer cheese scene, I noticed almost every beer cheese arrived supplemented with a pretzel. Besides Monnik's spent-grain bread, The Post's breadsticks, and Cumberland Brews jalapeños and Ritz crackers, every beer cheese I tried had a soft-baked pretzel for dipping. Gralehaus, Holy Grale, Four Pegs, and Bluegrass Brewing pretzels have the dark brown, Maillard-reaction color baked in; Craft House and Flanagan's serve chewier, lightly toasted pretzels. The former's pretzels puff up, while the latter's are stretched out.

Bardstown Road, in the Highlands neighborhood, is so flush with beer cheese joints that I'm naming it Beer Cheese Row. Morris' Deli sells their roughhewn, slow-burn beer cheese at Great Flood Brewing, whose beers pay deference to the Ohio River's record-breaking crest in 1937. Almost a mile down the road, River City Drafthouse bakes a massive pretzel that is served with either warm or cold beer cheese and crispy pita wedges. The cold version has a mustardy flavor, with smoky paprika dappled on top. Walk thirty-three feet to Cumberland Brews and try their russet-shaded beer cheese, which comes with a side of jalapeños. The beer cheese itself isn't zesty, so you'll need those peppers to add some heat. The spread is so compact, Ritz crackers break if you try to dip them.

Try an Irish version of beer cheese at Flanagan's Ale House, five minutes from Beer Cheese Row. They employ Guinness (naturally) in their smooth, peanut butter–hued beer cheese. Their beer list covers rarer beers from Chicago to North Carolina, and they have happy hour deals.

Close to the Highlands, the revitalized Germantown and Schnitzelburg neighborhoods (mentioned above) render even more beer cheeses. Four Pegs and The Post—both located on Goss Avenue—form what I'm calling the Beer Cheese Tandem. I can't recommend Four Pegs's beer cheese, unless you like your beer cheese to stick to the container instead of sticking to the pretzel. (It won't glom to the bread unless a utensil is used!) I'm not sure if it's supposed to be warm or cold—it looked like it had been semiheated, but it wasn't warm to the touch. Come here instead for their solid beer selection and to stare at a picture of *The Big Lebowski* characters posing as *The Last Supper.*

For real beer cheese, go next door to The Post, a New York–style pizza place located inside an old Veterans of Foreign Wars Post. Beer cheese is listed as a side and comes with garlicky breadsticks that balance the Coors beer, onion, and garlic in the peppery spread. The cracked and red pepper produces a thirty-second burn, so make sure you have a beer on hand to extinguish it.

From there, head downtown to Against the Grain Brewery and Smokehouse. Chef Jordan Delewis makes two kinds of cold beer cheese. The pinkish one comes with a greasy baked pretzel and a side of barbecue mustard; the second contains smoked gouda blended with an ATG beer and is served with kettle chips.

From brewpubs to German restaurants to Irish haunts to pizza places, beer cheese thrives in a multitude of Louisville eateries.

## Four off-the-Beaten-Path Things to Do in Louisville

### 1. See Kentucky Rushmore

All of the (dead) Kentucky greats—Muhammad Ali, Abe Lincoln, Colonel Sanders, Secretariat—star on the mural, nestled in an alleyway across the street from Beer Cheese Row, at 1583 Bardstown Road. Will Russell originally conceived the project to be a forty to sixty-foot-tall memorial, but the project got entangled in budget restraints. Instead, he commissioned Margaret Morely to paint the small mural on the side of his closed WHY Louisville store. It's a reminder of some of the larger-than-life legends that once inhabited the Bluegrass State.

## 2. Find Rare International Brews at Sergio's World Beers

More than a thousand beers live at this Butchertown beer store, running the gamut from rare American to Costa Rican brews, and touching on everything in between. The shop doesn't seem all that big until you realize it goes deep into other rooms. Sergio's also maintains an extensive draft list. (sergiosworldbeers.com)

## 3. Eat, Drink, and Shop Your Way through NuLu

NuLu, a four-block section of East Market Street, brings together all stripes of restaurants, shops, and bars. Wait in line at Feast BBQ, or try Central American cuisine at Mayan Café. Sample Decca's upscale farm-to-table provisions. For dessert, try the fresh bakery treats at Please & Thank You. Quench your thirst on Garage Bar's elaborate patio. Galaxie, a block away, serves tacos and mixes up pitchers of margaritas and cocktails; next door, Rabbit Hole Distilling covers all your bourbon needs. For a beer, stroll to Goodwood Brewing or Akasha Brewing Company. (nulu.org)

## 4. Play Pinball and Eat Pizza at Zanzabar

Part arcade, part bar, part restaurant, and part music venue, Zanzabar is a nonstop fun center. They book local and national bands and serve up homemade pizzas, a Hot Brown with beer cheese on it, and free-play vintage arcade games. Plus, they're located next door to Nord's Bakery, a stop on the Kentucky Doughnut Trail. (zanzabarlouisville.com)

# Cincinnati, Northern Kentucky, and Dayton

Because of the region's immense German population, most of the beer cheeses found in restaurants are of the warm variety. Dubbed Porkopolis, Cincinnati loves its pigs. Moerlein Lager House, located next to Great American Ball Park, pours warm beer cheese on pork-belly poutine. Their brewery in Over-the-Rhine serves a cold beer cheese spread with a soft pretzel made out of spent grain. But the beer cheese isn't spicy, or, for that matter, all that flavorful. Bistro Grace in Northside executes more of a gourmet effort with their flaxen-colored, warm beer cheese.

Wurst Bar in the Square, in Mount Lookout, makes Flying Pigs in a Blanket: dough-wrapped sausages served with a beer cheese dip. One of the more unusual beer cheese dips comes from Taste of Belgium (multiple locations).

They use a raspberry lambic beer in their dip, which tastes fruity. El Camino, a Latin-influenced eatery located near Wurst Bar, employs locally brewed MadTree beer in their beer cheese mac and cheese. Beer cheese finds its way onto Mac's Pizza's waffle-fry pizza; the beer cheese has a potent mustard flavor to it. Located at several locations throughout Cincinnati, Servatii Pastry Shop and Deli's spreadable beer cheese comes with a Bavarian pretzel. They even supply some bars in the area with the snack.

At the furthermost reaches of the beer cheese region, Dorothy Lane Market, a specialty grocery store with three locations in Dayton, Ohio, has made their own beer cheese for five years. Todd Templin's the VP of Beer, Wine, and Cheese at DLM. He told me their house-made cheese spreads sold well, so DLM's bakery director, Scott Fox—who had worked with a couple of chefs in Kentucky—and Templin thought beer cheese could sell well, too. "It does have a little of that Kentucky influence," Templin says. They add sour cream, a Wisconsin cheddar, red pepper, a dark European beer (Templin says "there's virtually zero alcohol in it"), and Tabasco, which gives it a tang.

"It's extremely popular," Templin says. "It's certainly among our top five cheese spreads." Because of its less expensive ingredients, their beer cheese is more cost-efficient than their other cheese spreads, like blue cheese and pecans, or smoked salmon spread. They make the beer cheese four times a week and sell it at all three stores. They stay ahead of the curve—I'm not aware of any other grocery stores in the area that make their own beer cheese. "We're always trying something new and unique and quick," Templin says. "You try to create things faster than your competition, if you will. We didn't see a lot of [beer cheese] going on in our area." Besides selling the beer cheese in an eight-ounce plastic container, they also sell it with pretzel trays, paying homage to the state's Teutonic heritage.

South of the Ohio River in Newport, Kentucky, Hofbräuhaus has several dishes made with beer cheese. (They also have locations in Cleveland and Columbus, Ohio; and Florida.) "The only reason we do that here is because when we first opened, we just had our pretzels and beer cheese [on the menu]," says John Ellison, general manager of Newport Hofbräuhaus. "But people loved the beer cheese sauce so much we added to some other items." Looking over the menu, I counted at least fourteen dishes with "bier cheese," including the traditional bier cheese and pretzel appetizer, bier cheese fries, and spätzle.

Wunderbar, in Covington, Kentucky, specializes in encased meats and also cultivates the best warm beer cheese dip in the Cincinnati region. Unlike a lot of beer cheese dips, this German restaurant's version is thick like a mushroom soup (but with pepper and Sriracha) and doesn't coagulate and form a film on top as it cools. A lightly colored, somewhat sweet and crusty house-made pretzel accompanies the beer cheese.

Warm beer cheese is fine, but to get the cold, Kentucky-style spread, visit the Tousey House Tavern, in Burlington, Kentucky (sixteen miles from downtown Cincinnati), which is one of the few restaurants in the area that has the cold dip on its menu. The upscale Southern restaurant is known for its fried chicken night, its selection of bourbon, and its beer cheese. Chef Jonathan Weiss created the recipe in 2008 when the restaurant opened. "Everybody usually has the hot, cheesy dip," he says. "When it gets hot like that, it gets unctuous and the cheese breaks down. Cold cheese holds up more for the batches we make." He shreds the cheese and then adds cream cheese, Samuel Adams beer, roasted garlic, Tabasco sauce, dry mustard, black pepper, cayenne, and "a couple little goodies in there to really make it pop." Weiss adds, "The cheese has to be shredded; otherwise it could have clumps and not have that smooth consistency." Once it's ready to serve, he'll dust fresh parsley on the top.

He makes about fifteen pounds a week and delivers twelve to fifteen orders a night. "We change our menu twice a year," he says. "That's just one of those things that stays there. It's one of the better things." Instead of just serving it with pretzel rolls, Weiss also adds sliced apples and grapes, for dipping. "If you've ever been to a Melting Pot, with their fondues they usually send out some stuff that you don't expect. Once you go with it, it's pretty good. I like apples and cheese. . . . It gives it that fresh taste, with the cheese." Weiss says he only sees the hot varieties in the Northern Kentucky/Cincinnati area. "Every place I go, it's always been hot, where you dunk your stuff instead of spreading it." But he notes some locations in Michigan serve a cold-style beer cheese. "It's like some places where you get chili and it's nothing like what you get around here." (Mudgie's Deli in Detroit offers a cold-style beer cheese made with white cheddar and served alongside pretzel rods. But instead of mixing the hot sauce into the spread, Mudgie's drizzles it atop the beer cheese.)

Like a lot of people I talked with, Weiss is dumbfounded as to why Kentucky-style beer cheese hasn't escaped Kentucky and its environs, though he speculates that the "outrageous" cost of cheese could be the culprit. "Cheese and bread are pretty good stuff," he adds. "I would like to see it go national. Maybe it'll catch on, and maybe people can do different variations of it."

## Wisconsin

Many people think Wisconsin is the origin of warm beer cheese dip and beer cheese soup, including Chef Kristin Hueneke, who creates a few beer cheese dishes for Lakefront Brewery in Milwaukee. She mixes up beer cheese to ladle over fries and to use in a soup. Lakefront teamed up with Uber Dairy and Wisconsin Cheese Mart for their version of "beer cheese," which consists of cheese curds soaked in Lakefront's coffee stout. The packaged label reads "beer cheese," but it's not what Kentuckians know—it's beer *and* cheese. If you threw their packaged cheese in a food processor and add some spices, then you'd have real beer cheese. "That was actually something that Wisconsin Cheese Mart sold me on," Hueneke says. "They brought in some samples. We thought it was really pretty with the marbling. It sells well at the Cheese Mart. There's already beer in it, so of course it's going to be good with beer." (Purchase your own from Wisconsin Cheese Mart's online store, and while you're at it, try Milwaukee Brewing Company's milk stout "beer cheese.")

Hueneke describes how Wisconsin-style beer cheese diverges from other regions. "It's typically got a heavy fat concentrate," she says. "Where whole milk is 3 percent [fat], Wisconsin people want 5 percent. [The resulting cheese is] nice and creamy. We know our cheese and we know our cheese palate. It's got a great mouth feel that's really going to accent the carbonation in the beer. That's why beer pairs better with cheese than wine does, because beer has the carbonation."

With the advent of the craft beer boom, some sort of warm beer cheese appears on a lot of brewpubs' menus, especially in Wisconsin. "You're kind of hard-pressed to find something in my menu that doesn't have cheese in it," Hueneke says. "We sell three hundred pounds of cheese curds per week. Very rarely do we get an order of fries that doesn't have the beer cheese added to it. While we're a German beer hall and while we're all about Wisconsin, our true thing is Milwaukee. That's why for the cheese curds we go to Clock Shadow Creamery. That's one of the only urban creameries in the whole state. That definitely reflects on the whole background of the city."

According to the National Historic Cheesemaking Center, Wisconsin cheese production dates back more than 185 years, to 1831. By 1910 Wisconsin surpassed Ohio and New York to "become number one in cheese production in the U.S.A." In 1950 the state processed 561 million pounds of cheese; by the twenty-first century, that increased to 2.8 billion pounds made at 126 plants. No wonder a lot of beer cheese makers source their cheeses from Wisconsin. (nationalhistoriccheesemakingcenter.org/history-of-cheese)

Hueneke doesn't know where the trend to feature beer cheese in brew-pubs began, but it obviously has roots in Milwaukee. "It's engrained in Wisconsin culture," she says. "Everybody's grown up with it. It's totally normal. Like I said, we know what a good cheese is, where other places are just like, 'Yeah. Cheese.' It's not the same. I'm pretty sure you can to a grocery store anywhere else and their specialty cheese selection is nowhere near what we have. . . . There's huge competition—ten different options for cheddars. I think that's specific to here, and that's something that's special about Wisconsin, and Milwaukee in particular, because we're combining the beer with it, too."

Despite the amount of beer cheese products produced in Wisconsin, cold beer cheese rarely shows up on menus. I'm guessing it's because, as Hueneke says, Wisconsinites love their high-fat content, and it gets cold up there. However, Merkts out of Stevens Point brands a line of beer cheeses made with local beers from Stevens Point Brewery and Capital Brewery; the spreads can be found in stores as far south as Northern Kentucky.

## Chicago

Chicagoans form another faction of midwesterners who are more habituated to warm beer cheese than cold. But in a sea of warm dips, a cold, smoky beer cheese emerges, courtesy of Chef Lamar Moore of Wicker Park barbecue joint Smoke Daddy. Owned by 4-Star Restaurant Group since 2004, the restaurant put beer cheese on the menu in 2005 (see recipe, p. 57).

"The ownership has done extensive recipe development in culinary classics, the beer cheese being one of them," Moore says. "The group as a whole decided on the recipe after doing research. Having the love for cheese, from being in the Midwest, they thought it would be great to have." Moore—who competed on an episode of the Food Network's *Chopped*—joined the restaurant in early 2015 and heads up the beer cheese making. He smokes jalapeños in a smoker for an hour, which is partially where the smoky flavor comes from. He also integrates pickled jalapeños, fresh jalapeños, a Wisconsin cheddar, Parmigiano-Reggiano, mayo, and a pale ale beer, and then serves a heap of beer cheese with tortilla chips. "Cold beer cheese is different from the rest because it has multiple layers of flavors," he says, explaining why they chose a cold spread over a warm one. The same beer cheese is served at bar and grill Dunlays on the Square, another 4-Star-owned restaurant, located in Logan Square. Smoke Daddy sells about twenty to thirty beer cheese orders a week. However, do Chicagoans understand what they're eating?

"Chicagoans are more familiar with warm [beer cheese], or their perception is it's a dip," Moore says. "A year ago we added a few new items on the menu, and we took our beer cheese, added some corn flour and other ingredients, to make pimento hush puppies with jalapeño jam."

Smoke Daddy isn't the only Chicago eatery that makes cold beer cheese. At the gastropub the Fountainhead in Lincoln Square, they make what they call a Wisconsin-style Pub Cheese: horseradish, Wisconsin Hook's cheddar, and

Stone Brewing pale ale, served with sliced pretzel bread and pickled veggies. The mixture is so spreadable it even comes with a spreader utensil. With Chicago's highest-in-the-nation sales tax added in, the "beer cheese" hits big-city sticker prices. Despite the cost, the Pub Cheese—in taste—inches closer to Kentucky beer cheese than Smoke Daddy's creation. Chicagoans don't seem to be clamoring for more beer cheese, but at least they acknowledge it.

# New York City

## *Floyd, NY / Union Hall*

One city that does comprehend beer cheese is New York, where you can get anything—including Kentucky-style beer cheese. Trailblazers Jim Carden and Andrew Templar introduced beer cheese to Brooklyn Heights in 2004 with their first bar, Floyd, NY. "I wanted to create a small business that we could use as a launching pad for other types of businesses," co-owner Carden says. "For me, music and programming were a big part of what I wanted to create, so starting off with something that was small and manageable was ideal." Carden and Templar grew up together in Lexington, then Carden moved to New York to attend New York University. After Templar graduated from Wittenberg University, he also found himself in NYC. He did a few odd jobs before his friend convinced him to venture into the bar business. "Jim had wanted to open a bar, and he started chatting with me about it, and then we began looking at rental properties and that's when we found the spot that became Floyd," Templar says. The name Floyd comes from a bar in Floyd, Iowa, named Floyd Y, that Carden and his wife once visited. "We fell in love with the place, so we created Floyd, NY," Carden says.

Ominous flea-market paintings of Ma and Pa Floyd hang in the bar above a full-sized bocce ball court that's situated in the middle of the bar area. Floyd beer cheese is the spreadable, solid variety, flecked with cayenne. Presented with a sleeve of Ritz crackers, this beer cheese needs a knife to slick it on the crackers, otherwise the crackers break when dipped. The crackers affix a nice crunch to the meal. Let's all give thanks to Brooklyn, because Floyd beer cheese is the most authentic version people will get outside of the Commonwealth. "Hall's, of course, was always a real favorite," Carden says. "We would go there and have it at the restaurant. That really was the one I thought was the best. That's kind of a consensus, probably." Floyd also sells Ale-8, another Winchester import, both in a Maker's Mark cocktail called Maker's 8 and in a longneck bottle. Basically, Floyd is a comforting reminder of Kentucky, seven hundred miles away.

"We wanted to provide something that we felt would be a good snack that people weren't that familiar with, and beer cheese was a perfect solution,"

Floyd beer cheese. (Courtesy Sam Horine)

Carden says. "We started experimenting and finding recipes that we liked. We had some from the family. Ours was very Kentucky and very much based on Kentucky recipes and influences. We definitely stuck to our roots."

"It was kind of rushed that we decided to do it, and so we just called our folks and said, 'Throw us some beer cheese recipes,' and a little trial and error is how we ended up with our final recipe," Templar says.

"We basically settled on one, and people really loved it," Carden says. "It was one of those products that just sold really well."

During the outset they'd use a Cuisinart located in their basement. "We'd hang up plastic on the ceiling so no dirt would fall down," Templar says. "It was very by the seat of our pants in the beginning."

Some research and development added butter to the beer cheese to keep it from crumbling, which turned out to be "ill-advised." They eventually settled on extra sharp New York State white cheddar, mixed in sharp yellow and extra sharp yellow cheddar, and then added Colman's Mustard powder, cayenne, garlic salt, white pepper, and a slightly flattened cheap domestic beer like PBR or Schlitz. "Beer cheese is so simple we didn't want everybody in the Northeast to realize they could make it themselves," Templar says, "so we tried to create an air of mystery around it."

New Yorkers are savvy and grasp the underpinnings of beer cheese. "People pretty much get it when you say beer cheese," Carden says. "Now, they don't totally get what it might taste like—there's a bazillion ways that you could go about something like that—but I find that from a communication standpoint it was such an easy sell, and people were instantly attracted to the simplicity of it. People find it really unique and different, and I think that people, especially in New York, really appreciate when a new food item has a history and a backstory the way beer cheese does. Occasionally we would have someone from Kentucky come in, and they immediately knew where they were." Beer cheese is the only food Floyd serves, but at the entertainment venue they also own, Park Slope's Union Hall, they serve the beer cheese with crackers and on a burger.

A few years ago, Carden, Templar, and their partner, Kevin Avanzato, launched Floyd Eats. They decided to retail their original beer cheese—along with a jalapeño one and a smoked bacon flavor. "We thought, well, let's try to sell our beer cheese nationally; let's try to do a food brand," Templar says. "How hard could it be? It was really challenging, especially a product like beer cheese, which is so perishable. I don't know how Hall's—I'm not sure how they do it with the real cheese." They worked with scientists from Ithaca to add the right amount of preservatives to the beer cheese, but it didn't taste the same as their bar versions. "When you add a preservative, you can't call it all-natural," Templar says. "It's always going to taste better fresh. So when we tried to go to market, it was hard to compete with restaurants that make it daily."

NYC's Union Hall makes a burger with beer cheese on it. (Courtesy Sam Horine)

"We had trouble on the manufacturing side," Carden says. "People responded to it well. We had it in a bunch of grocery stores here in New York. We had some in Texas. We never really went beyond New York City with the distribution. Because in order to do that, we would've had to produce larger quantities, and we just had a problem being able to create at those efficiencies where we could bring the cost down and make it worthwhile. We just were not able to take on larger-scale manufacturing. It was fun. It was a learning experience to try to do it retail." The retail business shuttered in 2015.

Although that business didn't launch, the guys still hoped their beer cheese would take off on a nationwide level. "When we did [performance venue] the Bell House, we'd have bands come through and we'd put it in the green room, and we hoped some rock outfit would fall in love with it and help spread the word," Templar says. "I don't know if that ever happened."

It didn't appear to happen. But Templar says in 2009 or 2010, he began seeing more restaurants in NYC doing beer cheese, because Southern food suddenly became all the rage. Floyd may not have catapulted beer cheese nationwide, but Carden and Templar innovated a special niche in the city. "I've had enough beer cheese for one lifetime," Templar says, "but I'm still a fan."

### Upright Brew House

At Perry and Hudson Streets lies the West Village's Upright Brew House. The brewpub serves their whipped beer cheese in a small jar surrounded by toasted baguette slices, similar to how Marion Flexner suggests in her recipe (p. 40).

They use Irish cheddar, an IPA, cream cheese, cayenne, and garlic, and then they dust chives on top of the finished spread. The cayenne makes the beer cheese burn for a few seconds. They don't make their own beers here but pour a wide variety of local and regional brews. For brunch, beer cheese comes on a breakfast sandwich called the Morning Melt, and—supposedly—for lunch and dinner they will make you an off-the-menu beer cheese grilled cheese sandwich.

## Earl's Beer and Cheese

Coast all the way to the Upper East Side and you'll find Earl's Beer and Cheese, the most out-of-the-way spot for beer cheese, unless you live near there. With beer and cheese in the restaurant's name, it's a no-brainer for Mike and Gina Cesari to serve beer cheese. The cozy gastropub complements its beer cheese with four or five local draft beers (hence the beer part in the name). Earl's also makes grilled cheeses, but for some reason sans the beer cheese. The beer cheese—served with a few crunchy, oily hunks of bread and two raw garlic cloves—contains chunky bits of New York State white and orange cheddar, doused with Sriracha, which supplies a kick. It'd make more sense if the garlic cloves were roasted, not raw, but the point is to rub the bread with the garlic.

The beer cheese comes in regular and jumbo sizes, and it's expensive compared to down-home offerings. With the exception of Floyd's cheaper-than-parking-priced-spread, be prepared to pay a little more in these big cities than you would in good ol' Kentucky.

## Three Non-Beer Cheese Things to Do While on the NYC Beer Cheese Trail

### 1. Play with Kittens

Located a block from Floyd, Brooklyn Cat Café allows cat lovers to pay a small fee to hug kittens and adult cats for an hour. Watch them run amok and gawk at turtles swimming in a fish tank. All of the cats and kittens are adoptable. Even if you're not in a market for a feline, playing with these cute animals offers an oasis of calm from the jungle—the urban jungle, that is. (Brooklyn; catcafebk.com)

### 2. Eat Cheese—but Not Beer Cheese—at Murray's Cheese Shop

You'd think a store that sells hundreds of cheese products would have beer cheese, but apparently they don't. Still, walk seven minutes from Upright Brew House to purchase local beers, gourmet chocolates, blocks of cheese, and sandwiches with cheese melted on them. (Greenwich Village; murrayscheese.com/greenwich-village)

### 3. Take in a View from Central Park

About an eight-minute trek from Earl's Beer and Cheese, on the Upper East Side of Central Park, sprawls the 1.58-mile Stephanie and Fred Shuman Running Track. Take a jog or gaze at a panoramic view of the Eldorado Building and the Jackie Onassis Reservoir. (Central Park, from 86th St. to 96th St.; centralparknyc .org/things-to-see-and-do/attractions/running-track.html)

# 6

# MAKERS AND BRANDS

Most of the retail beer cheese makers are family-owned enterprises run by only a few people. The beer cheese is made in a commercial kitchen, not in a factory or warehouse. People hand-stamp every container, add every sticker, and distribute the products to stores themselves. The craft movement—craft food, craft cocktails, craft beer—dovetails perfectly with beer cheese.

Most artisans, like Olivia Swan of Olivia's Beer Cheese, use some kind of cold-pack sharp cheddar. "The form that it comes in is much like the form that beer cheese ends up as," she says. "You would have to use a knife to get it out."

Every beer cheese product feels personal because you know someone painstakingly made it from scratch—and spent hours doing so. In fact, as you read this passage, these entrepreneurial artisans are probably making beer cheese. In buying beer cheese, understand you're a locavore supporting Kentucky Proud. So the next time you reach for that generic store-bought cheese spread, consider these and other beer cheese options.

THE BEER CHEESE BOOK

## Olivia's Beer Cheese

Olivia Swan didn't plan on becoming a beer cheese maven—but in 2012 it happened, after decades in the making. "My dad used to take us to Hall's on the River, and I just fell in love with beer cheese," Swan says. She considers her affection for beer cheese may have formed early: "When I was two, [my dad] gave me beer cheese and I liked it. I'm assuming it was mild," she says. In high school and college, the fixation continued, to the point she'd come home to Lexington and take containers of beer cheese back with her to Vanderbilt University in Nashville.

"Most Kentuckians don't know that beer cheese doesn't exist outside of Kentucky," she speculates. "I still talk to people all the time who say, 'They don't have beer cheese in Florida.' 'I know! Beer cheese is a Kentucky thing.' . . . For instance, when I went to Nashville, for college, I didn't realize that other people didn't care about Derby. People said, 'I don't know what the Kentucky Derby is.' Growing up, you don't realize that [your local culture] is unique until you step outside of it. Or maybe you didn't grow up in the culture, and you look at it and think, 'These Kentuckians are obsessed with this thing called beer cheese. I don't understand.'"

She describes beer cheese to outliers using a barbecue metaphor. "I always liken beer cheese to barbecue in that if you combine beer and cheese,

Olivia Swan of Olivia's Beer Cheese. (Courtesy Olivia's Beer Cheese)

A spread of Olivia's Beer Cheese. (Courtesy Olivia's Beer Cheese)

you should call it beer cheese. There's barbecue, and then there's Memphis barbecue, Carolina barbecue, Texas barbecue, Kentucky barbecue—and they're all very different takes on barbecue. That's how I see beer cheese. I've never had beer cheese outside of Kentucky that tastes anything like Kentucky beer cheese."

In 2006 Olivia and her dad started making beer cheese at home, and in 2010 a few friends who enjoyed her beer cheese encouraged Olivia and her dad to enter theirs in Winchester's second annual Beer Cheese Festival, in the amateur category. Much to their shock, they came in first. "I thought, you know what? Our friends weren't just being nice," she says. "This was legitimately good, as approved by the taste-testers of all the beer cheeses." By this time Olivia was living in Chicago and working in marketing. Her dad's office building in Lexington had a commercial kitchen, so Olivia, her brother, and her dad decided to channel their beer cheese ardor into a business, even if that meant Olivia would frequently have to commute almost six hours from Chicago to Lexington.

First, she had to pick the right base cheese, so she corralled twenty of her friends to sample different ones. "The cheese that you use is a big deal," she says. "Ninety-five percent of what's in there is the cheese, so if you change the flavor profile of the main ingredient you get a completely different tasting beer cheese." She chose a cold-pack cheese (and keeps secret what company makes it). "People are always sad when I won't tell them what's in it." The family makes sixty-pound batches at a time (or 125 eight-ounce containers), which takes about two hours—but that's just one flavor. Olivia makes mild, hot, and smoked versions; a rye whiskey beer cheese; a bourbon beer cheese; and seasonal variations. "One hard thing about starting the business was the number of beer cheese competitors. Why should I be successful if I do the same thing that everybody else is doing, like only making mild and hot beer cheese? I might as well not start a business. So I started doing different flavors of beer cheese, wondering: Is there something else that we're missing? Can I add another ingredient? Can I use whiskey?" She won't disclose what type of whiskey she uses, but she does make a special blend for Bulleit (from the Four Roses Distillery) using their bourbon. She also makes an exclusive recipe for Lexington's West Sixth Brewing using their IPA. "One of the best things I did was to approach West Sixth as they were getting ready to open. I said, 'I have an idea. You all make beer. I'm making beer cheese. What if I make beer cheese with your beer?' They thought it was an amazing idea, because their taproom doesn't have a kitchen. I do think that a beer that has a deeper flavor ends up making, in part, a better beer cheese."

West Sixth now has two locations, including their Greenroom, located downtown. Sunrise Bakery's baguette chips (see recipe, p. 47) accompany Olivia's beer cheese at the taprooms. Swan prefers to eat her beer cheese with potato chips, but her husband likes Wheat Thins. "I myself like a creamier beer cheese," she says. "I like to be able to dip a chip in and the chip doesn't break. I think that's one of the defining characteristics of Kentucky beer cheese: it's more a dip than hard. It's funny how particular people are about what they like to dip in their beer cheese."

Like almost everyone else, Swan guards her process; she's possibly even more tight-lipped than her competitors. "Because there are so many out there, keeping what you can a little bit secret helps to build the barriers around other people taking your recipe and just replicating it. . . . If I let all of my secrets and recipes be known, someone else could come in and do it more cheaply, be a copycat and put out a similar product, and then I don't have anything unique to offer anymore."

Kentuckians adore beer cheese, but Chicagoans? Not so much. When Olivia lived in the City of Big Shoulders she tried to sell her beer cheese to restaurants and retail outlets. "People said, 'Oh, I love beer cheese!' I'd reply, 'You don't know what beer cheese is!' So I learned to say, 'I bet you never had Kentucky beer cheese.' . . . 'Why is it different from something else?' In Chicago, if they don't have beer cheese on the menu, who cares. They don't know what they're missing. No one is going to request it. So when I left I wasn't too bummed."

In 2015 Swan left Chicago and moved to Cincinnati, and soon after she gave birth to her daughter. She still travels to Lexington once a week to make the beer cheese, but she's finding it difficult to keep up with demand. Jungle Jim's specialty food store in Ohio is one of her biggest clients. While we talked (and snacked on her beer cheese), she read an email from them requesting 720 containers. "Most people don't even order that in a year, and this is for the next five, six weeks. I don't know if can deliver all of it." It comes out to 360 pounds, and that's on top of her deliveries to West Sixth, other locales, and shipping the beer cheese as far as Hawaii. "I have as much work as I want, and I'm not trying to expand."

One appeal of retail-grade beer cheese is that most of them are hand-made locally. Olivia's Beer Cheese is a family-run business employing just three people. "Folks are shocked to learn that we don't have employees, and we don't have machines that automatically fill these containers," she says. "I sit next to the mixer with an ice cream scoop, and I scoop it in and put it on a scale and then pass it to my brother, and he puts on the lid. I hand-apply those labels, and I stamp those best-by dates on there, and then my brother puts the barcode labels on the bottom. Everything is hand processed." Nowadays, people take comfort in knowing someone handcrafted their provisions.

Unlike some other purveyors, such as Dad's and Key Ingredient, Swan only makes beer cheese, not nonalcoholic cheese spreads. "A lot of people ask me if I do other cheeses," she says. "I didn't start off as a chef. I don't know how to make anything else. I just learned how to make beer cheese, found out I was pretty good at it. That's all I know how to do, and it's kind of all that I want to do."

## Kentucky Beer Cheese

The name "Kentucky Beer Cheese" sounds like a catch-all, but it's one of the most recognized brands on the market. Sue and Jim Castano formed the company in 1987. "They had a part ownership in Johnnie Allman's at this time," Diane Evans, the current owner, tells me. "When it burned to the ground, the chef gave Sue the recipe, and she just made it for family and friends. At some point Jim bought her a big Hobart mixer, which we still use to this day." Once they went commercial, the Castanos vended their beer cheese in Kroger and other local grocery stores.

In 2004 health issues forced the Castanos to put their business up for

## Beer Cheese Scrambled Eggs and Omelets

Beer cheese pairs well with eggs. Whisk 2–3 eggs with a dash of milk and mix in three tablespoons of beer cheese. Sauté with veggies like onions, peppers, and mushrooms.

sale. "My husband had been looking for a business for us to buy, and usually he'd bring some business to light. When we heard [Kentucky Beer Cheese] was for sale we looked at it," Evans says. With a background in accounting, Evans crunched the numbers and knew it was a sure thing. "They were making money. There was lots of room for growth. So we bought it and I left my job and started running the company. From the time we bought it, we have more than quadrupled the sales. We have had consistent growth every year."

She now makes batches in her Nicholasville, Kentucky, facility, about twelve miles from Lexington. "Our recipe is strictly cold-pack cheddar cheese, domestic beer, and spices," she says. "Some recipes will include things like cream cheese or mayo or fillers to try and make it cheaper and bring the cost down. But it doesn't usually yield a consistent product. Ours is pretty pure."

They make about two thousand pounds a week, which fill four thousand containers. They ship the beer cheese as far as Oregon and California, but because it's perishable, it's difficult to ship anywhere that takes more than a couple of days of transit time, which rules out overseas sales. The Hobart mixer helps, and so does the pneumatic cup filler. Otherwise everything else is hands on. Why is Kentucky Beer Cheese so popular? "It's a very consistent product," Evans says. "We didn't try to have huge growth immediately. Sometimes growing too quick loses the quality of the product. It's a slow process to get people outside of Kentucky aware of it and for them to get addicted to it, but once they try it, usually they love it. Our recipe isn't overly complicated, and we haven't changed a thing from the original recipe." She says they sell more of the mild version than the hot, because "the word 'hot' does scare people. Our hot is not super hot. It's not chili hot. Our hot is a good hot, but there are people who like it even hotter."

Besides the mild and hot varieties, they also make a special version for lauded Lexington brewery Ethereal Brewing, which opened in 2014. "We know the people who own it [Andrew and John Bishop]," Evans says. "They live in the same neighborhood as we do, and our sons grew up playing soccer together. So when they were starting the brewery, they approached us. They picked different beers they wanted to try, and we experimented and found one that we thought had the best flavor." They use Ethereal's Lambda Oatmeal Stout in the beer cheese, which is sold in four-ounce and eight-ounce containers and served with pretzels. "The Lambda does alter the flavor slightly, but it's a good, different flavor. Sometimes you can bury the beer [in beer cheese] with normal domestic beers, so there's not going to be a huge difference in the flavor. But when you start getting into specialty brewing and richer beers, they give it a whole different flavor."

Outside the Bluegrass, Kentucky Beer Cheese has a distributor based in Michigan that allocates the product in Wisconsin, Illinois, Ohio, Indiana, Kentucky, Pennsylvania, Tennessee, and (hopefully) more markets soon. Evans says people outside of the state may have a Kentucky relative who's tried Kentucky Beer Cheese and suggested it to others. "Once they try it, they get hooked on it," she says. After making Kentucky Beer Cheese for more than twelve years, she doesn't get sick of it. "I still love eating it," she says. "I wish I didn't, because I could lose a little more weight that way."

To distinguish their branding from other beer cheeses, Evans designed a logo of a mouse holding a stein of beer in one hand and a wedge of cheese in the other; the product name appears on a blue silhouette of the Commonwealth. "The name is confusing to some people because they think we're just speaking generally," Evans said. "Sue trademarked [the name] in 1987. We added the mouse logo—I don't know how many years ago—just to give it a little more character, just to add a little bit to it. That was my goal: a cute mouse."

## River Rat Beer Cheese

Speaking of cheese-friendly rodents, in 1984 Bob Tabor started serving beer cheese in his Winchester restaurant, Engine House, and in 1999 decided to mass distribute it. In 2012 he asked Jenny Bailey, her husband H. R., and their kids to help more with the business. "I think we're one of the older ones," Bailey says. "After you [start making] bigger batches, the ratios kind of change, so that's why we still do it in small batches. We do everything by hand and just keep it small. I like stuff like that." River Rat orders their cold-pack cheese from Gordon Food Service and makes forty-pound batches at a time. "We make two hundred pounds per day," she says. "It takes three and a half hours to get it all mixed up. Then it'll take me [another] three and a half hours to package it. We make it one day, let it set overnight, and then package it the next day." Bailey claims letting it sit overnight improves the texture and consistency: "It lets air and gases out."

Bailey doesn't eat much beer cheese anymore, however. "I'll eat it every now and then," she admits. They don't use craft beer in their product. "Craft beers are great, but we're still just good ol' Budweiser," she says. "There are so many other varieties out there, the hybrids. Some people use cream cheese, some people use a shredded cheese, celery seeds. We just have the four ingre-

Jenny Bailey, co-owner of River Rat Beer Cheese, prepares a batch. (Photo by Steve Foley, courtesy *Winchester Sun*)

dients—simple and traditional." At one point, Bailey worked at Engine House and then founded her own restaurant called Bailey's Café; it no longer exists as a restaurant, but the location is now the base of operations for River Rat.

Since the advent of the Beer Cheese Festival in 2009, Bailey has noticed more commercial beer cheese makers flooding the market, which has led to more competition. "Before the Beer Cheese Festival, you could only find eight or ten beer cheeses on the market. After the festival, [there's] been a huge spike. Because now, at any time, there are probably sixty, seventy beer cheeses out there in the state of Kentucky." She thinks the market has become "too saturated" and admits that "it probably has hurt River Rat, to be honest." She adds, "We just have so many other beer cheeses out there that we're trying to compete with. I still think that we're one of the top [brands]; we're still a contender." (If it's any consolation, River Rat won second place in the commercial category at the 2015, 2016, and 2017 Beer Cheese Festivals.) Competition is especially fierce in Central Kentucky, and because River Rat doesn't have the marketing prowess of some of its competitors—they distribute the beer cheese themselves—the Baileys struggle to get it in stores outside of Lexington, Louisville, Bowling Green, and Winchester. "I would like to see it grow outside of Central Kentucky," Bailey says. River Rat would like to secure the Northern Kentucky territory but hasn't figured out how to break in. "We would like to expand our business, but at the ratio we do it, because everything's by hand, I don't know how much more I could do without having to hire a whole slew of people, and that would take away some of the quality," she says.

## Bell's Beer Cheese

Holly Rollins founded Bell's Beer Cheese in 2014, to stop her husband from henpecking her about her beer cheese. "I myself had always made beer cheese with my mother growing up," she says, "and we just made it for Christmas gifts. To tell you the truth, my husband nagged me for about twenty years before I decided to actually listen to him."

A couple of years ago she made a batch and delivered it to the now-closed Mason Liquor in Lexington. "They said if you make [beer cheese] into a business, we'll sell it, and so we started [the brand]." Started in 2014, Bell's—taken from Rollins's maiden name, not from Bell's Brewery—is one of the newer artisan beer cheeses on the market. "We're not that old, so we haven't grown by leaps and bounds," she says. "It's a second job for both of us at the moment, but we hope that one day at least one of us can run the business and one of us can go get some health insurance somewhere." When they aren't making beer cheese, Rollins is a social worker and her husband, Ben, works in medical bill-ing. Starting the business out of a commercial kitchen in Nicholasville came with a few curve balls. "We had to talk to a lot of lawyers," she says. "We had to go through several inspections, and just trying to figure out how to navigate that system was interesting. We're still learning. We did get a huge fine from the federal government the first year because we didn't fill out one piece of paper. But we were able to negotiate with them and filled out the right piece of paper. It's been a learning experience."

Rollins will only reveal she uses a lager beer and cheese purchased from Gordon Food Service. "We all go to the same place," she says. Why the Area 51–like secrecy, though? "Beer cheese doesn't have a lot of ingredients," she says, "so if you give any little bit away, you give away a secret. . . . Because obviously there's cheese and there's beer. There's not a lot of extra stuff in there, but all of us are required to have an ingredient label so you can see what's in it—but how we actually make it is very different."

The family recipe is at least thirty-five years old, and Rollins has been making it since she was a child. So when it came time to turn the recipe into an enviable business, she knew what to do. "Going into it we thought, it's easy to make beer cheese," she says. "We can do this. But you forget about having to make the labels, having to get all the ingredients, and all the other steps that occupy our time."

Similar to Full Circle Market, the Rollins sell a gluten-free version. "I had a friend at work who had a lot of family members with celiac," she says, "and they pushed and pushed. I truly tried to find them a company that was already making a gluten-free beer cheese, because there were a lot of steps to go through [to make my own], and I wasn't sure if I was ready. But I couldn't find anybody. So we found the right beer to make it with. We had it lab tested and went through inspection. It's got a little bit of a different taste, just because gluten-free beer tastes a little different, but it's not bad." (Bell's and Full Circle Market's gluten-free beer cheeses are sold at Lexington's Good Foods Co-Op.)

In the span of a few years, Rollins went from making her special beer cheese once a year to servicing the demand on a daily basis. "Everybody was wanting it," she says. "'Do you have any more? Can we get some? Are you coming to the potluck? Are you bringing beer cheese?' Now they can go to the store to buy it, so they don't ask me as much. 'Go get your own. It's not free anymore. I'm now trying to start a business, so you gotta help me out.'"

Rollins thinks beer cheese fetches so many followers because it's a Kentucky product. "We take a lot of pride in things that are from Kentucky," she says. "Most people that move into Kentucky from somewhere else have to experience beer cheese. After a while, they always have a lot of questions: 'What is this?' But if you're from Kentucky, you know what it is. You've grown up eating it." She's not sure why the dish isn't seen outside Kentucky's borders more, but she offers a valid reason. "I don't know if anybody's marketed and tried," she says. "I'm not too sure if anybody's tried to go that much farther. I've had friends who don't live here anymore who would love to see it. But if you think about it, Kentucky Ale-8 just recently went farther than Kentucky [in nationwide Cracker Barrel restaurants]. That means big shipping costs, and most beer cheese companies are pretty small. You're not talking about a huge manufacturer that has a warehouse."

In the meantime, Rollins will keep her company small and factory-free. Besides Good Foods Co-Op, Bell's Beer Cheese can be purchased from Lexington's Critchfield Meats; Discount Wine and Spirits in Edgewood, Kentucky; and Louisville's Baptist Health Hospital's cafeteria. Rollins and her husband would like to expand their beer cheese to bigger markets, but maybe not Kroger or Liquor Barn yet. "I don't know if we're ready to meet that demand," she says. "We hope to. I would like to see growth outside of Fayette County and get into some of the other markets that are out there. It would be nice to be able to hand the business down to our daughter, but we have a ways to go before that happens."

# RETAIL AND RESTAURANT GUIDE

## Retail Beer Cheeses

The following list names retail beer cheeses that are sold around Northern and Central Kentucky—ones I've seen sold in stores and ones that I know are currently active. (I may have missed a few, though.) You'll find them in behemoth liquor stores like Party Source, Party Town, and Liquor Barn, and some are sold at Walmart, but others are sold in specialty stores like Lexington's Good Foods Co-Op. Most of them are made in Kentucky, but I also include a few that are produced outside of the state but sold in Kentucky. Many of these out-of-state producers will ship their products all over the United States. Because they are retailed in mass quantities, you'll find the ingredients include extra things that aren't always found in restaurant and artisan beer cheeses: annatto coloring, guar gum, mold inhibitors, sodium phosphate, xanthan gum, and sorbic acid (a preservative). Other beer cheeses will add unnecessary fillers like high fructose corn syrup to lower production costs, so be sure to read the labels. In 2017 the average price for an eight-ounce container is $5–$6. (Howard's Creek hits $7.99.) Some beer cheeses are also sold in sixteen-ounce tubs. *(Unless otherwise noted, the places listed below are in Kentucky. Also, note businesses are subject to location changes and closures. Visit garinpirnia.com for updated information.)*

Allman's; Mount Vernon; allmansbeercheese.com

Ashby's Beer Cheese; various locations in Winchester and Florida; ashbysbeercheese.com

Beemer's; Lexington; facebook.com/beemersbeercheese

Bell's Beer Cheese; Nicholasville; facebook.com/bellsbeercheese

Big Poppie's Beer Cheese; Lexington (no website)

Big Russ; Beaver Dam; bigrussbeercheese.com

Brothers; Lexington; facebook.com/Brothersbeercheese

Brown's Tastee; Lawrenceburg; brownsbeercheese.com

Carr Valley Beer Cheese Spread; La Valle, Wisconsin; carrvalleycheese.com

Charlie's; Carlisle; charliesbeercheese.com

Colonel Coleman's; Winchester; colemansbeercheese.com

Colonel O'Kirby's; Winchester; okirbybeercheese.com

Copper Kettle; Louisville (no website)

Dad's Favorites Stampin Ground Beer Cheese; Lexington; dadsfavorites.com

Dorothy Lane Market Beer Cheese; 740 N. Main St./6177 Far Hills Ave./2710
Far Hills Ave., Dayton, Ohio; dorothylane.com

Hall's on the River; Winchester/Wisconsin; beercheese.com

Howard's Creek; Lexington; howardscreek.com

Judy Ann; Louisville; judyannselect.com

Kentucky Beer Cheese; Nicholasville; kentuckybeercheese.com

Key Ingredient Hot Horseradish and Ale; Bath, Pennsylvania;
keyingredientmarket.com

Larry Mac's; Lexington; larrymacsbeercheese.com

Mary Lou's; Lancaster; facebook.com/MaryLousBeerCheese

Merkts; Little Chute, Wisconsin; merkts.com

Mimi's Garden Fresh Beer Cheese; Shuckman's Fish Co. & Smokery, 3001
West Main Street, Louisville (no website)

Moo Shine; Versailles; mooshine.com

Morris' Deli; 2228 Taylorsville Rd., Louisville; facebook.com/
Morris-Deli-142048039162083

North Coast; Bowling Green, Ohio; facebook.com/NorthCoastBeerCheese

Olivia's Beer Cheese; Lexington; oliviasbeercheese.com

Ol' Man Ian's; Lexington; facebook.com/OlManIans

Pine River; Newton, Wisconsin; pineriver.com

PJ's Beer Cheese; Nicholasville; facebook.com/PJs-Beer-Cheese-
1770054539922091/

Red Clover; Louisville; rootedredclover.com

River Rat; Winchester; facebook.com/riverratbeercheese

Save-A-Lot Beer Cheese; Winchester; stores.save-a-lot.com/winchester-ky

Say Cheez; Lexington; facebook.com/SAY-CHEEZ-Beer-Cheese-
141062759407903

Scott's of Wisconsin; Sun Prairie, Wisconsin; scottsofwi.com

Tavern Cheese Spread; Tega Cay, South Carolina; facebook.com/
CheeseCreations

True Blue; Richmond (no website)

ValuMarket; several locations in Louisville; valumarket.com

Victory Brewing; Downington, Pennsylvania; victorybeer.com

Williams Cheese; Linwood, Michigan; williamscheese.com

## *Markets and Grocery Stores That Sell Beer Cheese*

Clifton Market; 319 Ludlow Ave., Cincinnati, Ohio; cliftonmarket.com

D.E.P.'S Fine Wine & Spirits; 424 Alexandria Pike, Fort Thomas; depsfinewine.com

Good Foods Co-Op; 455 Southland Dr., Lexington; goodfoods.coop

Jungle Jim's International Market; 5440 Dixie Highway, Fairfield, Ohio/4450
Eastgate South Dr., Eastgate, Ohio; junglejims.com

Kroger; several locations in Central and Northern Kentucky and Cincinnati;
Kroger.com

Liquor Barn; several locations in Lexington and Louisville; liquorbarn.com

Liquor City Uncorked; 501 Crescent Ave., Covington; facebook.com/
liquorcityuncorked

Liquor World; 239 Eastern Bypass; Richmond; facebook.com/liquorworldky

Lucky's Market; 1030 South Broadway, Lexington; 200 Hurstbourne Parkway,
Louisville; luckysmarket.com

Remke; several locations in Northern Kentucky and Cincinnati; remkes.com

Party Town; 6823 Burlington Pike, Florence; partytownky.com

The Party Source; 95 Riviera Dr., Bellevue; thepartysource.com

## Restaurants and Bars

Below is a list of restaurants and bars that serve beer cheese. *(Unless otherwise noted, these are Kentucky locations.)*

## *Kentucky and Ohio*

HARRODSBURG AND DANVILLE

Beaumont Inn / Old Owl Tavern / Owl's Nest Lounge; 638 Beaumont Inn Dr.,
    Harrodsburg; beaumontinn.com
Beer Engine; 107 Larrimore Ln., Danville; facebook.com/
    Beer-Engine-131855603494793

LEXINGTON

Chatham's; 496 E. High St.; chathamsscf.com
Country Boy Brewing; 436 Chair Ave.; countryboybrewing.com
Limestone Blue; 133 N. Limestone; limestoneblue.com
The Julep Cup and Seahorse Lounge; 111 Woodland Ave.; thejulepcup.com
O'Neill's; 2051 Richmond Rd.; oneillslexington.com
Parlay Social; 249 W. Short St.; parlaysocial.com
Red State BBQ; 4020 Georgetown Rd.; redstatebbq.com
Saul Good; 123 N. Broadway/3801 Mall Rd./1808 Alysheba Way; saulgoodpub.com
Smithtown Seafood; 501 W. Sixth St.; smithtownseafood.com
West Sixth Brewing; 501 W. Sixth St. #100/109 W. Main St.; westsixth.com
Windy Corner Market; 4595 Bryan Station Rd.; windycornermarket.com

Retail and Restaurant Guide

Against the Grain; 401 E. Main St.; atgbrewery.com

Bluegrass Brewing Co.; 300 W. Main St.; bbcbrew.com

Crescent Hill Craft House; 2636 Frankfort Ave; crafthousebrews.com

Cumberland Brews; 1576 Bardstown Rd. (no website)

Eiderdown; 983 Goss Ave.; eiderdown-gtown.com

Flanagan's Ale House; 934 Baxter Ave.; flanagansalehouse.com

Four Pegs; 1053 Goss Ave.; fourpegsbeerlounge.com

Gralehaus; 1001 Baxter Ave.; gralehaus.com

Great Flood Brewing Co.; 2120 Bardstown Rd.; greatfloodbrewing.com

Holy Grale; 1034 Bardstown Rd.; holygralelouisville.com

Monnik Beer Co.; 1036 Burnett Ave.; facebook.com/Monnikbeer

The Post; 1045 Goss Ave.; thepostlouisville.com

River City Drafthouse; 1574 Bardstown Rd.; rivercitydrafthouse.com

NORTHERN KENTUCKY AND SOUTHERN OHIO

Bistro Grace; 4034 Hamilton Ave.; Cincinnati, Ohio; bistrograce.com

El Camino; 1004 Delta Ave.; Cincinnati, Ohio; facebook.com/elcaminocincy

Hofbräuhaus; 200 3rd St.; Newport; hofbrauhausnewport.com

Longfellow; 1233 Clay St.; Cincinnati; https://www.longfellowbar.com/

Mac's Pizza Pub; several locations; macspizzapub.com

Moerlein Lager House, 115 Joe Nuxhall Way, moerleinlagerhouse.com;
	Christian Moerlein Brewing Co., facebook.com/christianmoerlein

Servatii Pastry Shop & Deli; several locations; servatii.com

Taste of Belgium; several locations; authenticwaffle.com

Tousey House Tavern; 5963 N. Jefferson St.; Burlington; touseyhouse
	.com

Wunderbar; 1132 Lee St.; Covington; facebook.com/wunderbar.covington.3

Wurst Bar in the Square; 3204 Linwood Ave., Cincinnati, Ohio;
	wurstbarinthesquare.com

WINCHESTER

Blue Isle Home-Style Restaurant and Bar; 5 Shoppers Dr.; facebook.com/
	Blue-Isle-Home-Style-Restaurant-and-Bar-1662944523988945

DJ's Bar and Grill; 836 Bypass Rd.; facebook.com/DJsSteakHouseBarandGrill

Engine House Deli and Pub; 9 W. Lexington Ave.; facebook.com/
	enginehousedelipub

Full Circle Market; 240 Redwing Dr.; fullcirclemarket.com

Gaunce's Deli; 845 Bypass Rd.; gaunces.com

Graze Market and Café; 150 Combs Ferry Rd.; facebook.com/grazelex

Hall's on the River; 1225 Athens Boonesboro Rd.; hallsontheriver.com

JK's at Forest Grove; 4636 Old Boonesboro Rd.; facebook.com/
JKsAtForestGrove

Woody's Sports Bar and Grill; 923 Bypass Rd.; facebook.com/
Woodys-Sports-Bar-and-Grill-108989639155441

Waterfront Grille and Gathering; 220 Athens Boonesboro Rd.; facebook.com/
Waterfront-Grille-and-Gathering-124740924265667

## *Up North*

Chicago

Fountainhead; 1970 W Montrose Ave.; fountainheadchicago.com

Smoke Daddy; 1804 W. Division St.; thesmokedaddy.com

New York City

Earl's Beer and Cheese; 1259 Park Ave.; earlsny.com

Floyd, NY; 131 Atlantic Ave.; Brooklyn; floydny.com

Union Hall; 702 Union St., Brooklyn; unionhallny.com

Upright Brew House; 547 Hudson St.; uprightbrewhouse.com

WISCONSIN

Lakefront Brewery; 1872 N. Commerce St.; Milwaukee; lakefrontbrewery.com

MICHIGAN

Mudgie's Deli; 1300 Porter St.; Detroit; mudgiesdeli.com

# ACKNOWLEDGMENTS

To my family: my mom, my brothers Reza and Bob, my sister-in-law Dawn, my nephew Blake, and cousins Gary and Suzi Kraus, for believing in me and supporting me.

To my cat, Diablo, for being a cuddly distraction and source of much-appreciated warmth and fun. (He does not like beer cheese, though.)

To my dad, who once told me, "Writing is the most talented thing a person can do."

To Adam, for being my chauffeur, barista, personal chef, beer cheese taster, personal assistant, photographer, map maker, and for his endless support in telling me I could write this damn book.

To every editor I've ever worked with: thank you for taking a chance on me and for challenging and educating me and pushing me to do better work.

To Ashley Runyon, for "discovering me," and for giving me the opportunity to write this book.

To Sara Bir and *Paste Magazine*, who let me write about beer cheese in the first place. And for creating the best-ever beer cheese cupcake recipe.

# Acknowledgments

To Nancy Turner, for spending an entire day driving me around the Beer Cheese Trail—and for being an all-around great person.

To California State Northridge and Ohio University, for teaching me the fundamentals of writing and filmmaking and sparking my interest in those subjects.

To Prince Rogers Nelson, David Bowie, Muhammad Ali, Gene Wilder, Leonard Cohen, Sharon Jones, Florence Henderson, Carrie Fisher, Debbie Reynolds, George Michael, Bill Paxton, and Harambe the Gorilla, who all died while I was writing this book. Your inspirations live on.

To coffee and tea, for giving me the right amount fuel I needed to write this thing. It was either coffee and tea or Adderall.

To sleep, which is my favorite thing to do when I'm not writing or drinking coffee or playing with cats.

To the kind people of Kentucky, whose hospitality is unsurpassed.

To the baby raccoons I saved while writing this book, and to Robin Thompson of Nature's Haven, who gave them the life they deserved.

To Netflix and Spotify, for being both good and bad distractions.

To my former Chicago MyOpenBar staff, for being good (and bad, but mostly good) influences, both personally and professionally.

To the cities I've lived in: Chicago; Studio City, California; Temecula, California; Centerville, Ohio; Covington, Kentucky; Athens, Ohio; for helping to shape who I am.

To NYC, whose beer cheese gave me an overdue excuse to visit one of my favorite cities.

To the University Press of Kentucky, for the life-altering opportunity, and for granting me permission to use a couple of recipes previously published in *Out of Kentucky Kitchens* by Marion Flexner (2010) and *The Kentucky Fresh Cookbook* by Maggie Green (2011).

To UPK's editors and peer reviewers, for getting the manuscript into good shape.

To the Kenton County Library, for having such a great collection of Kentucky cookbooks.

Visit garinpirnia.com for more information.

# INDEX

*Page numbers in italics refer to photographs.*

# Index

Index

Index

Index

Hot Mess sandwich, 68
Hougen, Richard T., 17
House Recipe Wafers, 70
Hueneke, Kristin, 133–36

jalapeños: chopped, 17; nachos, 32, 109; pickled, 58–59, 102; side of, 126; smoked,
    57–59, 137; soaked in beer, 98; type of beer, 96
Jane Barleycorn's, 121
Jim Beam Nature Preserve, 117–18
JK's at Forest Grove, 71–73
Johnnie Allman's restaurant, 1, 3, 157
Johnson, Karl, 5–6
*Jonathan's Bluegrass Table: Redefining Kentucky Cuisine* (Lundy), 19
Julep Cup, 111
Justus, Jennifer, 20

Keeneland Racecourse, 112
Kenny's Farmhouse white cheddar, 45, 122. *See also* cheddar
Kentucky Beer Cheese, xi, 106, 110, 157–60
Kentucky Derby, 12, 16–17, 150
*Kentucky Derby Museum Cookbook,* 16–17
Kentucky for Kentucky, 113–14. *See also* Fun Mall
*Kentucky Fresh Cookbook, The* (Green), 20, 45–46
Kentucky Horse Park, x, 112
*Kentucky Keepsakes* (Ross), 18
Kentucky Native Café, 113
Kentucky Proud, 88, 92, 149
Kentucky River, 1, 61, 79, 118
Kentucky Rushmore, 127

# Index

# Index

Index

# Index